SUPER-SOLAR HOUSES

Saunders's Low-Cost, 100% Solar Designs

William A. Shurcliff

(With extensive help from Norman B. Saunders)

Brick House Publishing Company
Andover, Massachusetts

Published by Brick House Publishing Co., Inc.
34 Essex Street
Andover, Massachusetts 01810

Production Credits:
Book design: Wilson Graphics & Design (Kenneth J. Wilson)
Cover design: Mike Fender
Editor: Jack D. Howell
Copy editors: Linnea Leedham Ochs and Rich Garcia
Typesetting: dnh Typesetting

Printed in the United States of America
Printing 9, 8, 7, 6, 5, 4, 3,

Library of Congress Cataloging in Publication Data

Shurcliff, William A.
    Super-solar houses.

    Bibliography: p.
    Includes index.
    1. Solar houses.   2. Solar energy—Passive systems.
3. Saunders, Norman B.   I. Title.
TH7414.S49 1983   690'.869   83–2495
ISBN 0–931790–48–4
ISBN 0–931790–47–6 (pbk.)

CONTENTS

ACKNOWLEDGMENTS

I owe a great debt to Norman Saunders for explaining to me, in great detail, the designs of the three houses. Understanding came hard, but he persevered in his explanations and, at last, I obtained a reasonably complete understanding of the underlying inventions, the general rationales of the solar heating and cooling systems, and the important details of materials and construction that are prerequisite to high performance and low cost. Also, I am indebted to him for allowing me to use some of his excellent photographs. Finally, I am indebted to Robert Bushey, owner of Shrewsbury House, and Antonio Pulsone, owner of Cliff House, for allowing me to publish detailed accounts of their houses.

Chapter 1

INTRODUCTION

This book is about three remarkable houses. One, called Shrewsbury House, was essentially completed and occupied late in 1981; through two winters and one summer it has performed with full success. Another, called Cliff House, is nearly complete as of this writing (May 1983). The third, called All-Solar-Too House, is a design prepared for the 1982 Gardenway Passive Solar Design Competition; as yet no construction is scheduled.

MAIN PERFORMANCE FEATURES

All three houses, employing unique solar heating systems invented and engineered by Norman B. Saunders of Weston, Massachusetts, are 100% solar heated. More exactly, they are kept warm by intrinsic heat sources (human bodies, electric lights, cooking stove, etc.) and by solar energy. None has a furnace or wood stove. Also, all stay cool in summer.

The "100% solar heated" claim needs some slight qualification. Although the houses will remain comfortable throughout the winter without auxiliary heat, the occupants may, on certain occasions, make use of a small electric heater to make one room extra warm, as for example, if someone in the house is ill, or to accelerate the drying of fresh paint. And they may do so when, for experimental purposes, various changes are made in system components or in control procedures. One house, Cliff House, has a fireplace that was included for reasons of esthetics.

All three houses have many attractive features other than heating self-sufficiency. Operation is automatic, or nearly so. The houses remain fairly warm in winter even if left unoccupied for a week or more. Each has an integral south greenhouse or sunspace. Each has ample window areas, not only on the south, but also on the east, west, and north.

In each of these houses, the space heating system employs no conventional collector panels, no pumps, no valves, no drains, no moving liquid, no pipes. There are no Trombe walls. In none of the living-area rooms is there any bulky equipment used solely for space heating; thus there is great freedom of choice in room layout, furniture placement, etc.

All three houses have automatic passive solar preheating of the domestic hot water supply.

LOW COST

For each house, construction cost is low—about the same as for a conventional house of comparable size and comfort. More interestingly, the construction cost is comparable to, or slightly lower than, that of a typical 40–80% passively solar-heated house, and is much lower than that of a typical *actively* solar-heated house.

How can the cost be so low? Because:

- Most of the components consist of low-cost materials—air, water,

stones, glass, plastic, fiberglass, etc.

- Most of the components can be assembled on-site by carpenters and others of typical competence.

- There is no furnace, no oil tank, no furnace room, no furnace chimney, no radiators, no air conditioner.

Operating cost also is low—$50 to $100 per year for electric power to run the one or two small fans that are the heart of the temperature control system.

COMPARISON WITH OTHER LEADING DESIGNS

How do these three houses compare with other outstandingly successful, energy-conserving passive solar houses in the United States and Canada? It is premature to make judgments with respect to Cliff House and All-Solar-Too House. But Shrewsbury House has been in use throughout two winters and one summer, and the record is clear: its performance has been superb. I make the guess that its performance equals or surpasses that of all other houses—in the USA or Canada—of comparable size, comfort, etc.

Many hundred superinsulated houses have been built and operated for one or more years and have performed excel-

lently. They keep warm in winter and cool in summer. But nearly all of them require an auxiliary heating system. Most have no greenhouse. Many require operating thermal shades in the evening and in the morning. Many have smaller-than-normal areas of windows on the east, west, and north sides of the house.

Scores of double-envelope houses have been built and operated for two or more years. They have performed well, and annual fuel bills have been of the order of $200 or less. But auxiliary heating systems are needed and some rooms are sometimes on the chilly side. Many double-envelope houses entailed considerable extra construction cost, of the order of \$5,000 to \$15,000. (Some early builders of double-envelope houses have recently lost some of their enthusiasm for the double envelope itself and are attaching greater significance to earth-coupling and solar-energy storage—a shift toward some of the features that, in Saunders-designed houses, play major roles.)

About 100,000 passive solar houses that have large areas of south-facing windows and much added thermal mass have been built and have been in use for two or more years. Nearly all of these require auxiliary heating systems; many require large areas of thermal mass that preempt space in the most important part of the house—the south part; many employ large thermal shutters or shades that must be operated twice a day; many suffer from excessive glare on sunny days; many tend to overheat, especially on very hot days late in the summer when the solar energy input via the south windows is especially large.

Clearly it is a noteworthy advance when a solar engineer develops designs that, besides requiring no auxiliary heating system, provide an integral greenhouse, have ample window areas on all sides of the house, operate automatically (no thermal shutters or shades to operate), reduce glare, keep cool in summer, and solar-preheat the domestic hot water supply. To do all this at a cost that is no greater than that of a conventional house is a landmark achievement. The performance of the Shrewsbury House is now well proven, and I am confident that Cliff House and All-Solar-Too House have the capability of approximating its superb performance.

CRUMBLING OF THE CLASSIC RULE, "DO NOT TRY TO ACHIEVE 100% SOLAR HEATING"

Ten years ago, most solar architects and engineers were convinced that, in designing houses for cold climates (such as New England), it was foolish to try to achieve 100% solar heating. Prestigious experts made detailed calculations that showed conclusively (they said) that, in New England for example, it was unwise to try to achieve more than about 50 to 70% solar heating. They warned that the cost of achieving a higher percentage, such as 80 or 90%, would be enormous and would far outweigh the benefits. Even if the designer were to double the size of the collector and double the size of the storage system, he would get only about 90% solar heating. To achieve 100% might require tripling the sizes, and much of the added capacity would be useful only on five or ten days a year.

Especially clear warnings against attempting to achieve 100% solar heating in cold climates are contained in articles by G. O. G. Löf and R. A. Tybout. See, for example, their article in *Natural Resource Journal*, Vol. 10(2), p. 268, 1970, or their article in *Solar Energy*, Vol. 14, p.

253, 1973. Tybout was an economist and Löf was one of the world's foremost solar heating experts. (In 1974 I wrote to both of those men, trying to persuade them to take a more optimistic view, but in vain.)

Faith in the experts' negative pronouncements began to weaken a few years ago with the advent of superinsulated houses. By 1981 there were hundreds of such houses, and by the spring of 1983 one or two thousand had been completed or were under construction in the USA and Canada. Most of these houses require only $50 to $150 worth of fuel per winter, and a few come close to being 100% heated by the combination of intrinsic heat and direct-gain solar energy. Many such houses have no furnace, but do have a wood stove or a small electric heater.

The final crumbling of the experts' gloomy view occurred in January and February of 1982. In those midwinter months, Robert Bushey, owner and occupant of Shrewsbury House, found that his house held at about 70°F—day and night, in clear weather and overcast weather, with no back-up heat at all. The goal was reached: 100% solar heating in a cold climate! It was reached at no extra cost. For good measure, the goal was achieved without turning the thermostat that controls the fan below 70°F, without reducing the areas of east, west, and north windows, without needing to close thermal shutters each night and open them each morning, and without curtailing fresh-air input.

WHY A FULL-LENGTH BOOK?

To devote an entire book to three solar-heated houses may seem absurd. A typical solar house can be described in a few pages.

But Saunders's three low-cost, 100%-solar houses are different—very different. They embody several radically new approaches to solar heating. The design goals and also the general strategies used are new and strange, and some of the key components are puzzling even to experienced solar designers.

A galaxy of new concepts is involved.

To clearly convey what the designs are all about, and what exactly the heating and cooling systems consist of, requires a book.

NORMAN SAUNDERS: INVENTOR AND DOER

Norman B. Saunders, a professional engineer residing at 15 Ellis Road, Weston, MA 02193, is a thoughtful, quiet, deliberate inventor: an inventor of the lone-wolf type and one of New England's best-known solar consultants.

His passion is devices that are simple, homely, and durable. He avoids like the plague any device that is merely brilliant, flashy, impressive, or striking. From forty years' experience in physics, mechanical engineering, electrical engineering, and electronics engineering, he has developed the greatest distrust of "brilliant" devices which, so often, turn out to cost three times as much as anyone had predicted and to break down much too promptly.

He turns his back instantly, with no apology, on most types of conventional solar heating equipment.

Ignoring popular trends in solar design, he goes his own way, trying to formulate the heating and cooling requirements in the simplest and most basic way possible.

One of his main approaches is to use a multipronged attack: use a lot of "little" pieces of equipment that will work together well. Each, although simple and unimpressive, contributes significantly. Together they provide a full but low-cost solution.

Accordingly, his inventions cover a broad range, from special glazing materials and special window structures to special south-roof louver systems, special heat-storage assemblies, and special airflow controls; also, various special systems for use in commercial buildings, e.g., high-temperature (steam-producing) systems. (The appendix lists many of his patents.)

But he does a lot more than think and patent: he tries out his inventions promptly. He puts them to work, either in his own house or in houses of friends or clients. Often he continues to improve a given invention, year after year.

Some of the solar houses that he has designed—and that have worked well—are described in my earlier books. See for example the following books that are listed in the bibliography: S–235–t, pp. 130, 131, 132; S–235–aa pp. 98, 124, 127; S–235–cc, pp. 44, 76; S–235–ee, p. 95. His first solar house is described in his book *Solar Heating Basics*, bibliography item S–26, and in a very recent report (S–27–m). See also the book by Carriere and Day, C–85.

I have found his patents hard to read, hard to understand. My impression is that few people have given the patents the attention they deserve. He has written a number of reports on his inventions, but they are heavy reading.

For all these reasons, his major contributions to the art of solar heating have been, until now, little known outside of New England. This is true even though he has been generous with his time in presenting papers on his developments at various meetings of solar energy societies and in giving monthly talks and seminars to local groups on the theory and practice of solar heating.

SOME WARNINGS

Possible Errors

Some errors may occur in this book. No reader should place full reliance on any statement without obtaining formal confirmation from an authoritative source.

Design Limitations

Some of these design features are tentative, or experimental; shortcomings may come to light in the future.

Nothing presented in this book is intended to imply that the designs are final or are of assured success in all respects. The book guarantees nothing. It merely constitutes a serious effort to describe my understanding of the houses in question, and to make the account available *now*—not two years from now when performance data will be firmer.

In no sense does this book take the place of, or substitute for, detailed architectural drawings and specifications. The book is focused on the rationales, the principles, the general layouts, and the general modes of operation, not on detailed dimensions and detailed methods of construction.

Because each design employs many strategies and many components, all chosen to suit the outdoor temperatures and amounts of sunshine at the particular site and suit the size of the proposed house, such design will probably *not* suit other locations and other house sizes. For different sites and different house sizes, different specifications are required.

Patents

Some of the key features of the houses are covered by patents held by Norman B. Saunders. In some sections of the book I call attention to some of the pertinent patents, but in other sections I have not attempted to do so. I understand that Saunders will welcome inquiries as to the obtaining of licenses to build devices covered by his patents, and I have been impressed with how small his license charges are.

The mere fact that a person owns a copy of this book, or that this book presents descriptions of patented devices, constitutes no right or permission to build a patented device—even for one's own use—without first obtaining a license from the patent owner.

Some of the special names used for devices invented by Saunders are trademarked. In some instances I call attention to the existence of trademarks.

The appendix lists pertinent patents and trademarks.

Chapter 2

PREVIEW OF THE THREE HOUSES

LOCATIONS AND STATUS

Shrewsbury House, in Shrewsbury, Massachusetts (a few miles northeast of Worcester), was essentially complete by the end of 1981. It has been occupied continuously since then. It has performed well; all major goals appear to have been achieved.

Cliff House, in Weston, Massachusetts (about 12 miles west of Boston), is not quite complete. As of May 1983, some interior work remained to be done and the solar heating system was not complete—although it was already sufficiently operative to keep the house fairly warm, even with the house unoccupied and not having any intrinsic heat. Extensive calculations by the designer convince him that the goals will be met; he is confident that the house will go through the winter without auxiliary heat and will go through the summer without need for an air conditioner.

The All-Solar-Too House exists only on paper. There is as yet no undertaking to construct it. Again, the designer's calculations form a reasonable basis for the conclusion that such a house, like the two mentioned above, will go through the winter without auxiliary heat and will go through the summer without need for an air conditioner.

GENERAL DESIGN

Shrewsbury House is a two-story, split-level house with an integral greenhouse and integral two-car garage. Total floor area, including greenhouse and garage, is 2,860 sq. ft. The integral greenhouse is intended for serious use in growing plants in all but the coldest months; its design (with full south glazing, full overhead sloping glazing, and use of *single* glazing in order to maximize solar transmission) is such that, typically, plants grow here about as well as they would grow outdoors in full sunlight— or *better* than outdoors, if account is taken of the higher indoor temperatures.

Shrewsbury House. General view showing integral greenhouse, glass-covered south roof, and two-car garage.

Cliff House. General view showing house proper, sunspace, and two-car garage.

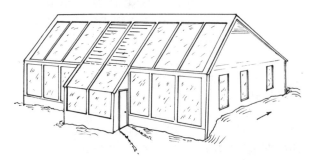

All-Solar-Too House. General view, showing glazed south roof, glazed south vertical face, and integral greenhouse that serves also as an air-lock entrance.

Cliff House also is a two-story house. But here the greenhouse is better called a sunspace; it is intended more for general living than for growing plants. Sixty percent of the south face of the sunspace is transparent (glazed); the glazing is double and has a transmittance of about 80%. There is no solar aperture in the attic: all of the solar radiation that enters the house enters via the vertical windows of the sunspace or of the living region. Circulation of air to or from the upper storage system or lower storage system is forced by an especially versatile *two*-fan system. The two-car garage is on the east side of the house; it was placed here because the only feasible location for the driveway is on the east; accordingly the garage is not in position to block the prevailing west wind of winter.

All-Solar-Too House is a small (1000 sq. ft.) one-story house with no garage. It includes a small (8 ft. × 6 ft.) greenhouse that serves also as an air-lock entrance. Emphasis is on:

low cost of contruction—about $50,000, or $50 per sq. ft.;

maintaining a uniform near–70°F temperature throughout the winter with no need for auxiliary heat; maintaining temperatures in the 70°F to 80°F range in summer with no need for an air conditioner;

steady intake of fresh air, using energy-scavenging preheating;

high percentage of solar heating of domestic hot water—60% to 100%;

a modular and highly flexible design such as could be applied to one-story houses of different shapes and sizes.

NOTE: A detailed comparison of the three houses is presented in chapter 25.

SIMILARITY OF GOALS

Goals vs. Strategies

Goals and strategies are two different things. *Design goals* are the general kinds of results that the designer hopes to achieve. *Design strategies* are the general approaches, or means, of achieving the goals.

In describing these three Saunders-designed houses, it is important to list the goals clearly and fully. Proper choice of goals is half the battle. A large part of the ingenuity of design of these houses is the ingenuity brought to bear in choosing the goals. (Probably some solar designers have been careless in setting goals: perhaps they have "taken the goals for granted" and concentrated on mere implementation.)

Main Goals

In designing these three houses, Saunders's main goals were to provide 100% solar heating, uniform temperature control throughout the house, automatic operation, and true cost-effectiveness.

100% solar heating All heat that is not supplied by intrinsic sources (human bodies, electric light bulbs, cooking stove, etc.) is to be supplied by the sun. Room temperature is to be kept at about 70°F. Even in week-long cold, cloudy spells in midwinter, there is to be no need for a furnace, or wood stove, or electric heater. Even if the amount of in-trinsic heat is greatly reduced, as by replacing ordinary refrigerators, cooking stove, lights, etc., with newer models that use less energy, there is to be no need for an auxiliary heat source.

Uniform temperature control throughout the house All of the rooms, not just the south rooms, are to be kept at about 70°F. There is to be no "making do" with 60°F in north rooms or bedrooms or utility rooms, and no allowing of big temperature differences between first-story and second-story rooms.

Automatic operation In winter the solar heating system is to operate fully automatically. There is nothing for the occupants to do: no need to check on indoor or outdoor temperature, or sky condition, or weather prediction; no need to open or close doors, windows, or thermal shades (there are no thermal shades). The system should be sufficiently self-balancing and have such a reserve of heat, that—even if all the occupants are away for a week for more—room temperature will remain at about 70°F. Also, the greenhouse should never get too hot and never get as cold as 32°F.

True cost-effectiveness The cost of constructing the house is to be about the same as (possibly less than) that of a conventionally heated house of comparable size and comfort.

The annual cost of power for operating the solar heating sytem is to be minimal: say $50–$100.

The annual maintenance cost likewise is to be minimal.

Other Goals

Window areas on all four sides of the living region of the house are to be ample.

The living region is to be free of Morse (Trombe) walls and other thermal storage systems. The solar heating sytem must not impinge on the esthetics of the living region.

Glare, which could be bad inasmuch as the south window area is large, must be controlled.

All the windows of the east, west, and north walls of the living area must be openable—to provide ample cross drafts in summer.

There are to be no restrictions on colors of floors and walls, or on coverings on floors or walls. There is to be no requirement that the living area floors be free of rugs and be of dark color. Floors and walls may be entirely normal in every respect.

Humidity must be controlled. Throughout the winter the relative humidity in the living region of the house must be kept below 50%.

There must be a steady inflow of fresh air—at least 80 cfm even in the coldest weather.

The rooms must remain reasonably cool in summer, i.e., about 70°F to 75°F most of the time, and no hotter than about 80°F even in long hot spells. There is to be no need for an air conditioner.

The domestic hot water supply is to be solar-preheated.

The garage (if any) is to be kept at least reasonably warm by solar energy.

The greenhouse or sunspace is to be warm enough in summer, spring, and fall so that plants can be grown there successfully in those seasons. In winter the temperature there must never fall below 32°F.

There are, of course, various other goals that are special to each house. These are discussed in later chapters.

SOME CONTRASTS WITH OTHER TYPES OF SOLAR-HEATED HOUSES

Other types of solar-heated houses are designed with very different goals in mind, as discussed below.

Ordinary Direct-Gain Passive Houses

Direct-gain passive houses are popular and successful. They are comfortable, provide good thermal performance, and may be economical.

But they have serious limitations:

The designer does not seek 100% solar heating, and acknowledges that a furnace and/or wood stove will be needed.

The room-temperature goal may be 60° or 65°F rather than 70°F. Even lower temperatures may be tolerated in long cold spells. Less-used rooms may be allowed to cool down to 55°F. North rooms may be permitted to be colder than south rooms—or may be "written off" as useful only as utility, vestibule, or storage space.

The occupants may feel obliged to adjust sliding doors, operate thermal shutters and shades, etc. They may feel they need to keep close watch on outdoor and indoor temperatures and on weather predictions. When the prediction is for a long, cold cloudy spell, they may be somewhat apprehensive. If they are away for a week or two in midwinter, large excursions in room temperature may occur.

The floors of south rooms may have to be dark and bare.

In some south rooms, glare may be excessive.

Glare may be excessive in south rooms because the south window area is so large and may be excessive in other rooms if such rooms have only one small window each (unilateral fenestration).

There may be no provision for avoiding excessive humidity in the rooms.

The greenhouse, if any, may threaten to cool down below 32°F unless a large array of thermal shades, auxiliary heat, or a special thermal storage system is provided.

The humidity in the greenhouse air may be unpleasantly high on some occasions—because of the lack of a steady supply of outdoor air.

Excessive temperature swings in the greenhouse may threaten to produce smaller but objectionable swings in the adjacent south rooms.

Solar energy may or may not contribute to domestic hot-water (DHW) heating.

In summer, the south rooms may receive too much solar radiation—especially if the south roof includes skylights, which sometimes receive more energy than can be concurrently vented there.

In summer, cross drafts through the rooms may or may not be provided.

Ordinary Indirect-Gain Passive Houses

Many of the limitations listed above apply to indirect-gain passive houses also.

In addition, south rooms may be greatly encumbered by Trombe walls or water-filled tanks. These restrict the view, block daylighting, preempt valuable space in the most important region of the house (the south region), may sometimes become too cold and sometimes too hot, and may give out heat to the rooms even when the rooms are already too hot. Also, to avoid excessive loss of energy through the big south window area, the designer may have to provide thermal shades here, and these may have to be operated every morning and evening. Trombe walls do a poor job of supplying heat to north rooms. In a cold cloudy spell they supply heat throughout a short period only, such as one night.

If a solar sunspace or greenhouse is provided, many of the limitations pertinent to the direct-gain approach apply. A sunspace can supply much heat to the rooms when they are already hot enough or too hot, but it may supply little or no heat to the rooms when heat is most needed there, i.e., in a long, cold cloudy spell. The amount of heat supplied to north rooms may be very small unless a special fan and control system are provided. If the sunspace is used as a greenhouse, its air may be very moist; flow of moist air to the rooms is often welcome but under some circumstances can make the room air too moist. If there are open doorways between the sunspace and the rooms, greenhouse insects may enter.

Superinsulated Houses

Superinsulated houses are rapidly growing in popularity. They certainly provide much comfort, require very little auxiliary heat, and are extremely economical to build and operate.

But they have these limitations:

The designer seldom achieves 100% solar heating. A wood stove is often provided; perhaps a furnace also, or a small electrical heating system.

Below-70°F temperature may be accepted, especially in north rooms or less-used rooms.

Thermal shades may be required.

Window areas are not generous. They are "normal" at best, and somewhat below normal at worst. Daylighting and view through the east, west, and north windows is normal or somewhat subnormal.

A steady stream of fresh air may or may not be provided. Humidity may or may not be kept below, say, 50%.

There is ordinarily no greenhouse.

Cross drafts in summer may not be ample.

Intrinsic heat plays such an important role that:

a. If lower-energy types of refrigerator, cooking stove, electric lights, etc., were used, a real problem would arise: More auxiliary heat would be needed.

b. If the family is unusually small or the house is unusually large, more auxiliary heat may be needed.

c. If the family is away for a week or two in midwinter, it may find on return that room temperature is unacceptably low.

Solar energy may or may not contribute to DHW heating.

Double-Envelope Houses

A moderate number of (a few hundred) double-envelope houses have been built and many of them have performed well. Rooms are usually comfortable and the auxiliary heat requirements are small. The occupants have, in the main, been pleased with the thermal performance.

But such houses have these limitations:

100% solar heating is not achieved. A wood stove is usually provided. Electrical heating is also often provided.

Too high a temperature in upper-story rooms may sometimes have to be accepted, and too low a temperature in some lower-story rooms may sometimes occur if the occupants fail to invoke auxiliary heat.

Window areas on the east, west, and north must be curtailed, reducing daylighting and view.

The occupants may feel obliged to pay close attention to room temperatures and to the weather—and to operate sliding doors, vents, etc., as appropriate. Knowing how to optimize such controls may take experience and skill.

Solar energy may or may not contribute to DHW heating.

If the occupants go away for a week or two in midwinter, they may find on return that some of the rooms are too cold.

The double-wall feature of such houses may entail much additional cost—not only for lumber, etc., but also for fireproof lining sheets, automatically closing fire-stopping dampers, damper reset controls, etc.

A detailed analysis has been made of one near-standard type of double-envelope house; see bibliography item G–182. The investigators found that, although the house in question performed well on the whole, the main convective loop actually exhibited little flow of warm air to the earth beneath the lower story; little energy was stored in that earth on a typical sunny day; and, often, auxiliary heat was needed. The investigators listed several design changes that might be expected to considerably improve the thermal performance of the house. Several of the suggested design changes are, interestingly enough, strongly in the direction of key features that have long been advocated by Saunders.

Earth-Sheltered Houses

These houses are popular in some parts of the country—especially where tornadoes are a threat. Earth-sheltered houses are more or less tornado proof. They are comfortable the year around. The annual heating bills are small. The houses are durable, and maintenance requirements are minimal. Direct-gain solar heating plays a big role.

But there are these limitations:

100% solar heating is not achieved. Usually a furnace or a wood stove is provided.

There may be no windows (or at best a few) on the east, west, and north. Thus daylighting and view may be drastically limited.

Unless great precautions are taken, ground water may present a problem.

Pressure from the flanking earth masses is so great that very thick and strong concrete walls may be needed. Also, the roof may have to be very thick and strong to support its earth load. A roof-edge fence or guardrail may be needed.

Usually it is practical to have one story only (with no basement or attic). Thus an unusually large area of ground is needed to provide a given amount of useful floor area. Also, much space is preempted by earth berms.

Because the south face is nearly all glass, and because all visitors, tradesmen, etc., approach the house from the south, such persons may be free to look into every room. Privacy is minimal, unless large-area curtains are drawn.

Cross drafts in summer may be small or nonexistent, unless special provision for ventilation is provided.

Solar heating may or may not contribute to DHW heating.

The limitations are spelled out in some detail in my article in the September–October 1980 issue of *Earth Shelter Digest*; see bibliography item S–235–ff.

Chapter 3

GENERAL STRATEGIES

Now we switch from goals to strategies and consider how the goals are to be attained. What general strategies, approaches, rationales, and ploys are available to the designer?

Listed below are the general strategies that, as I see the situation, Saunders used in planning the heating and cooling systems for the three houses in question. I regard this set of strategies as the most interesting part of the book.

Two strategies are of paramount importance: a *broad-spectrum* strategy and a *double-duty* strategy.

BROAD-SPECTRUM STRATEGY

Stress *variety*. Use a broad spectrum of devices—a multiprong attack. Employ a great variety of components and processes that are carefully matched to one another so as to work together cooper-

atively, each making up for the limitations of others. Each may be simple, inexpensive, and not especially impressive; but together they provide superb performance.

DOUBLE-DUTY STRATEGY

Stress *true integration* and *double-duty function*. An attic south roof, if properly designed, can serve not only to shed rain but also to admit solar radiation. Attic insulation can serve not only to insulate the house in general but also to insulate an upper thermal storage system. Insulated foundation walls can serve not only to support the house but also to contain and insulate a lower

thermal storage system. Vertical south windows, if properly designed, can serve not only for admitting light and view but also for air-thermosyphoning collection of solar energy. A single fan can serve not only to drive hot air from an upper storage system to a lower storage system but also to supply warm air to a greenhouse and drive stale air to the outdoors via an air-to-air heat ex-

15

changer and induce a corresponding in-flow of fresh air. Making major components of the house do double duty saves money, saves space, and minimizes complexity.

For many years designers of passively solar heated houses have given lip service to the integration of house and solar system. They say, for example, "House and solar collection and storage systems should be one and the same. Complete integration is the key to success!" But all too often, they backslide: they install artificial Trombe walls or artificial water-filled tanks at the south side of the living room, or they construct sun-scoop clerestories to bring solar radiation into north rooms. All too often they regard any component that is included, or is adjoining, or operates passively, as being integrated.

Contrariwise, much of the integration employed in Saunders's three houses is true, intimate integration. For example, in the Shrewsbury House the south roof *is* a huge solar window; the attic and its contents *are* the upper thermal storage system; the living room south windows *are* the thermosyphon collectors.

OTHER GENERAL STRATEGIES

Many other strategies are available. All of the strategies given below are employed in Shrewsbury House and many (but not all) are used in Cliff House and All-Solar-Too House.

Taking the greatest pains to reduce heat loss. This applies to the opaque wall and roof area, the building foundations, and the glazed areas of the walls and roof. (Later chapters discuss use of barriers against moisture and infiltration, use of double barriers, and use of negative pressurization.)

Providing two large thermal-capacity storage systems: one above the upper story and the other below the lower story. The living space is thus sandwiched between an upper warm region and a lower near-room-temperature region.

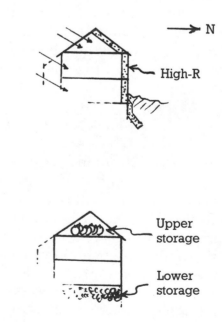

Keeping the upper storage system at a temperature well above room temperature by: (1) arranging for some objects well above room temperature to receive and absorb solar radiation, and (2) largely thermally isolating this storage system from the rooms below so that those rooms will not become too hot.

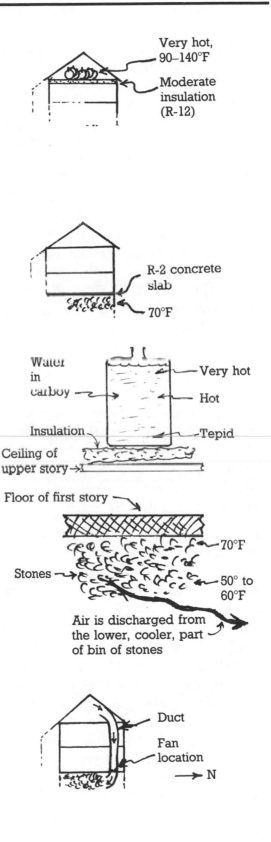

Keeping the lower storage system at, or slightly below, room temperature, and providing a moderate amount of thermal conductance between this storage system and the rooms immediately above it.

Maintaining thermal stratification within the upper storage system—so that the uppermost part may be very hot and may store much heat and the lowest part may be relatively cool and accordingly needs little insulation between itself and the rooms below.

Maintaining thermal stratification within the *lower* storage system—so that although the uppermost part is at about 70°F and thus helps control the temperature of the rooms above, the lowest part may be at only 50° or 60°F with the consequence that the flow of air from this part to the greenhouse entails loss of *low*-grade heat only.

Maintaining (and automatically regulating the speed of) an airflow from the upper storage system to the upper part of the lower storage system, so that the former will keep the latter at about 70°F.

Providing the capability of changing quickly and automatically from *heating mode* to *cooling mode*—as for example in spring and fall when the outdoor temperature may change from 45°F to 90°F or vice versa within a period of a day or two. The upper storage system is at all times "ready and waiting" to supply heat, and the lower storage system (at about 70°F) is at all times "ready and waiting" to provide cooling if the room temperature threatens to rise well above 75°F. Thus the system has at all times an *aggressive dual capability* of supplying much heating and much cooling within a period as short as 48 hours.

Protecting all, or part of, the south window area of the house proper with a thermal buffering zone (greenhouse) kept warm during the day by solar radiation and kept above 32°F at night by 50°F to 65°F air discharged from the lower (cooler) part of the lower storage system.

Including, in any large south window area that receives much solar radiation, a sheet that absorbs a substantial fraction of the incident solar radiation, and provide flanking air channels that permit the heat from the two faces of such a sheet to be transported into the upper storage system by air thermosyphon. Thus (1) eliminate glare, (2) avoid overheating the south rooms on sunny days, (3) provide R-value high enough to considerably reduce heat loss on cold nights, and (4) supply heat to the upper storage system.

(Most of the individual strategies listed above contribute to this capability.)

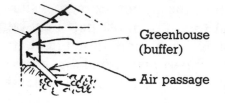

Greenhouse (buffer)

Air passage

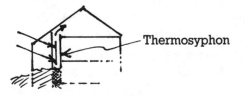

Thermosyphon

Including, in every other large window area that receives much solar radiation, a sheet that transmits a large fraction of the visual component of solar radiation and reflects almost 100% of the middle and far infrared, i.e., radiation in the range from 1 or 2 microns to 40 microns and beyond. The effective R-value of the window is thus more than twice that of an ordinary double-glazed window.

Arranging for the system to be self-regulating, so that (during most of the winter, for example) the house occupants have no responsibilities as far as temperature control is concerned.

Making sure that all of the components are simple, reliable, and inexpensive, and are easily transported, assembled, and installed.

Remembering at all times the threat of overheating in summer. Making sure that the chosen components and operations are helpful not only in winter but also in summer.

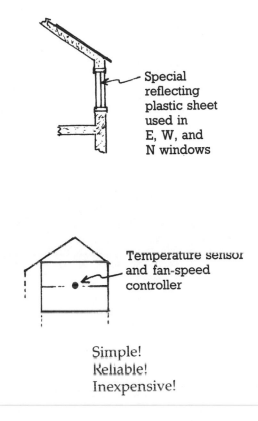

Special reflecting plastic sheet used in E, W, and N windows

Temperature sensor and fan-speed controller

Simple!
Reliable!
Inexpensive!

I
SHREWSBURY HOUSE

PHOTO BY DAVE SOUZA

Chapter 4

SHREWSBURY HOUSE: SPECIFIC STRATEGIES

Shrewsbury House is situated on a slight rise in a generally flat and sparsely populated region of Shrewsbury, Massachusetts, about 35 miles west of Boston. It is a fairly windy location: there are no tall trees close to the house.

It is a 6,800-degree-day (Fahrenheit) location.

This is a two-story, split-level, wood-frame, three-bedroom, two-bathroom house with an integral greenhouse and integral two-car garage, a full-length at-

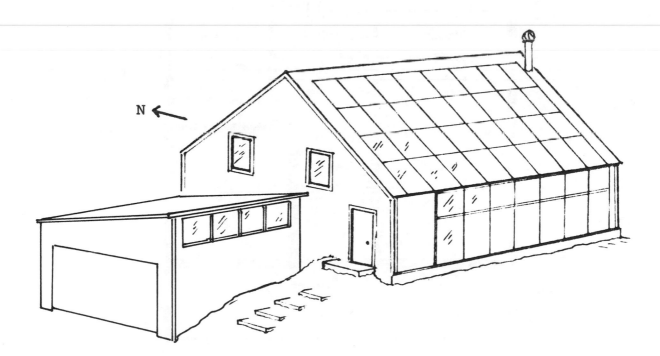

General view, showing the integral greenhouse, glass-covered south roof, and two-car garage.

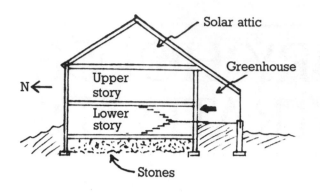

Simplified cross section, looking east.

tic, and no basement. The floor area of the living space alone is 2,200 sq. ft. Including the greenhouse, the area is 2,450 sq. ft. Including the garage, the area is 2,860 sq. ft.

It is based on an architectural design by John Davies and was constructed in 1981 by Violette Brothers of Shrewsbury.

The cost in 1981, not including the land, architect's fee, or solar designer's fee, was in the neighborhood of $90,000. The cost *including* all fees but not land was about $98,000.

The following drawings show the general layout of the house. The upper and lower stories have essentially the same room layout—a feature that would permit dividing the house into two apartments (upstairs, downstairs), for two families.

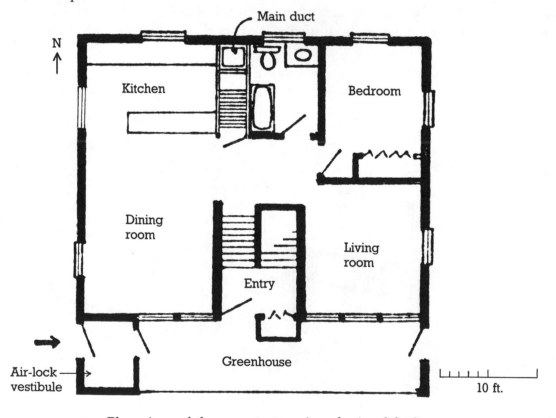

Plan view of the upper story (much simplified).
The greenhouse is at a slightly lower level.

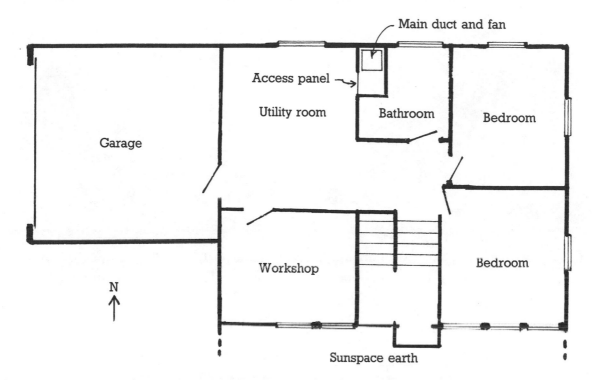

Lower story (much simplified). The floor level of the
living area is 3 ft. below the greenhouse ground level.

View showing the main entrance door, also the main
garage door. The insulation on the projecting portion of
the greenhouse south foundation wall is clearly visible.

West end of the house. Note the vent in the upper region of the greenhouse and two vents in the west main gable.

View of the south and east faces of the house. The east face includes four windows and the greenhouse east door.

Greenhouse interior, looking southeast. Note the 6-in.-wide trough beside the sill.

View from the upper southwest room, looking south southeast.

View showing the west and north faces of the house. The
two-car garage is partly solar heated. At the extreme left,
the duct for intake of outdoor air in summer is visible.

View showing the north and east faces of the house. The
duct for outdoor air intake in summer is clearly visible.
There are six north windows and four east windows.
Clapboard siding is used.

Interior of the upper-story southwest room. There are no eaves to block daylighting or the view upward to the south.

View showing some of the closely packed, water-filled, 6-gal. carboys in the attic.

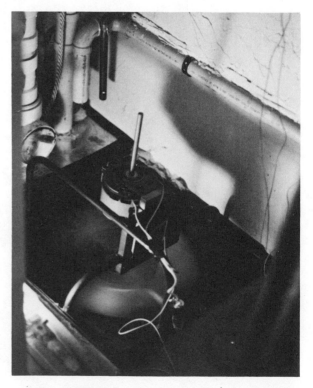

The ¼-HP fan is located near the floor level of the lower story.

View showing part of the living room (upper story southeast
room) and greenhouse. The big vertical posts are extra
heavy to support the trusses that carry the load of the 18,000
lb. of water in the attic storage system.

View from the lower-story southwest room. All four south
rooms have tall, full-width window areas.

The general goals and strategies of all three houses have been detailed in the previous chapter. Now I turn to the implementing strategies used in Shrewsbury House. These too are novel, interesting, and crucial to the overall success of the house.

The strategies are given here in broad terms only. Detailed accounts, with specifications of materials, dimensions, etc., are presented in later chapters.

The specific strategies pertain to:

upper solar energy collecting and storing system (attic system);

lower thermal storage system (bin of stones);

greenhouse;

air-drive system;

and many other systems, most of which are (like the above) special, but some of which are routine, i.e., nonspecial.

UPPER SOLAR ENERGY COLLECTING AND STORING SYSTEM (ATTIC SYSTEM)

The strategy is to provide an upper solar energy collecting and storing system that includes an attic solar window and upper storage system.

Attic Solar Window

This window occupies most of the area of the south-sloping roof and, in this area, *is* the roof. It has such a large area that, on sunny days in winter, it transmits an enormous amount of solar energy—of the order of 100,000 Btu/hr., or 500,000 Btu per sunny day.

This window has such a high thermal resistance that the amount of solar energy collected on a sunny day is order-of-magnitude greater than the nighttime heat loss through this window. Even during a cold and fully overcast midday hour the amount of solar energy collected (from the diffuse radiation) exceeds the amount lost through this window during this hour.

The window structure includes a set of reflective near-horizontal louvers that enhance the direct-solar-energy-intake in winter and reject nearly all such radiation in summer.

The window uses such inexpensive components and requires so little labor that it costs far less per square foot than typical collectors, and may cost only about twice as much as an ordinary shingled and insulated roof.

Some additional features of the attic solar window are that it has no moving parts, is very durable, and requires little or no servicing for at least twenty years. It is high enough above the ground so as to avoid being shaded by nearby trees.

Upper Storage System

This system employs enough water to provide large thermal capacity, so that the solar energy received (via the attic solar window and the vertical thermo-syphoning windows) on a sunny day will not raise the temperature of this thermal mass by more than 30°F.

The containers used:

- are transparent and thus admit solar radiation directly to the (water) contents;

- are of such size that the total quantity will have an aggregate surface area great enough (about 2,000 sq. ft.) for heat to flow rapidly *to* the containers from hot air rising from the thermo-syphoning window systems during the day, and *from* the containers to the attic air at night;

- are (when empty) so light that they are easily carried by hand;

- are sufficiently short and broad-based that no special stands or supports are needed; they may sit directly on the attic floor;

- are sufficiently corrosion-resistant that one may use, as thermal mass material, ordinary water—water that contains no additives for controlling pH or inhibiting corrosion; the expected lifetime of the containers is at least 50 years.

The storage system occupies no valuable space—no space in the upper story or the lower story (attic space is considered low-value space).

No special insulation is required on the four sides or overhead. The insulation on the attic gables, attic north roof, and the (transparent) attic south roof suffices.

Only a little insulation is needed beneath the attic floor. Because the lowest part of the storage system is the coolest part of the attic (thanks to the existence of some thermal stratification within the water-filled containers and also within the attic air as a whole), a small amount of insulation between the attic and the room below suffices, especially inasmuch as a small downward flow of heat helps keep the upper-story rooms warm.

The system contains a domestic hot-water tank and a high-up supply line (serving that tank) that is long enough to pick up much heat from the very hot air surrounding it.

The attic can be kept from becoming too hot in summer by opening one or more vents in the east and/or west gables.

There is free access (clear walkways) to all components.

NOTE: The thermal mass is small enough, relative to maximum loads that snow and wind can impose, so that the added support strength needed adds only slightly to the cost. Note also that the flow of solar energy to the upper storage system and the extraction of energy from that system make use of no moving parts whatsoever and no ducts, pipes, fans, blowers, dampers, etc.—aside from the air-drive system that serves the lower storage system (see page 34).

LOWER THERMAL STORAGE SYSTEM (BIN OF STONES)

Here the strategy is to provide a lower thermal storage system that consists of a bin containing 100 tons of stones.

The bin has such a large heat-transfer surface (air-to-stones surface area of the order of 200,000 sq. ft.) that it can extract heat from an incoming hot-air stream at a reasonably high rate (such as 100,000 Btu/hr.) even when the temperature difference (ΔT) is only one Fahrenheit degree.

It has many times greater thermal capacity (per degree of temperature rise) than the upper storage system, thus can store a comparable amount of heat with many times smaller temperature rise. Thus the excursions from 70°F will seldom exceed a few degrees.

The bin extends beneath the entire concrete-slab floor of the lower story, thus can supply heat to all of the lower-story rooms.

Input and output passages are sufficiently extensive that the flow of air reaches all regions of the storage system with approximately equal effect.

The bin has sufficient depth that, if warm air enters the bin near the top and eventually leaves near the bottom, an appreciable amount of thermal stratification will occur. Such stratification is helpful. Heating the lower-story rooms is favored over heating the greenhouse, and only the lowest grade of heat (e.g., 50° to 60°F air) flows to the greenhouse.

The system has such a large aggregate cross section of air pathways (of the order of 50 sq. ft.) that the pneumatic resistance is negligible—less than 0.1 inch of water.

- It employs no special container, no special support, no special insulation. These are provided by the ground below and by the insulated foundation walls.

- It serves as support for the concrete-slab floor while the floor is being poured and while it is hardening.

NOTE: The storage system employs the cheapest and most durable solid material known: stones. They are expected to perform well, with no maintenance, for more than 100 years.

GREENHOUSE

Another strategy is to provide an integral greenhouse that extends along the full length of the south side of the house.

It is tall enough to adjoin and buffer the south faces of both stories.

It is about half as wide as it is tall, so that much of the solar radiation entering the greenhouse will strike and enter the south windows of the living area.

An air-lock vestibule is located at the end most used (near the garage and parking area). A simple door is at the other end, and an inner door leads to the house proper.

The earth is deep enough that the plants will continue to grow well even if they are not watered for several weeks.

The greenhouse is fully glazed, both on the south vertical face and the sloping roof. The roof contains no opaque region such as is employed in some greenhouses in order to reduce over-heating in summer.

The roof has the same slope as, and is coplanar with, the south sloping roof of the house proper. Thus these two expanses of glazing join smoothly to form a single large glazed area.

Single glazing is used. Thus the amount of solar radiation actually entering the greenhouse is remarkably large. Losses by reflection and absorption are remarkably small. Consequently,

1. the plants in the greenhouse grow especially rapidly; and

2. the amount of solar radiation reaching the windows between the greenhouse and south rooms is especially large, which facilitates daylighting, direct-gain solar heating in the rooms, and air-thermosyphon heat collection as explained in chapter 10.

Also, single glazing is cheaper than double glazing.

To a considerable extent, the greenhouse is thermally isolated from the contiguous rooms, although closely coupled to them optically.

As support for the vertical south glazing, there is a concrete foundation wall, the south (outdoor) face of which projects 1½ to 2 ft. above the outdoor ground level and thus receives much solar radiation. It is insulated with transparent plastic sheets and airspaces and provides these benefits:

1. The upward-projecting part of this wall receives and absorbs much solar radiation, but loses little heat to the outdoor air; accordingly, it contributes to preventing the greenhouse air temperature from falling as low as 32°F at night.

2. Enough heat is stored in this wall, in the greenhouse earth, and in the earth beneath an adjacent outdoor, below-grade insulating panel or skirt, so that no earth close to this wall gets as cold as 32°, no freezing or frost heave can occur, and accordingly it is permissible for this wall not to extend down so deep as would normally be required—with resulting saving of money.

The 1½ to 2 ft. projection of the greenhouse south foundation wall plays an additional role relating to snowfall. When there is a snowfall, some pile-up occurs at the base of the south greenhouse face; and although the snow shades the above-ground portion of the foundation wall, it does not shade the greenhouse glazing. Incidentally, the insulating plastic sheets are very tough—tough enough to withstand falling hunks of ice and thrown stones.

In the lower central region of the north wall, an opening permits forced air (air that flows from the lower part of the lower storage system and is at a temperature well above 32°F) to flow into the greenhouse and keep its temperature well above 32°F. Because on a sunny day this forced air is colder than typical air already in the greenhouse, this air spreads throughout the base of the greenhouse and thus helps, with its slightly greater than normal content of CO_2, the transpiration of the plants growing there.

Along the base of the vertical south glazing, a trough collects some of the cold air that descends close to that glaz-ing on the indoor side and can guide some of this cold air to the inlet end of an exhaust duct. (This duct, which also fulfills a heat-exchange function, is discussed in chapter 9.)

At each end there is a large (summer-use) vent situated near the top of the greenhouse, so that the hottest air can escape easily. Each vent cover is manually opened about May 1 and closed about November 1. (Automatic actuators were installed, but were found not to be necessary and were removed.) When the vents are open, the prevailing west wind can cause a strong flow of air through the greenhouse.

AIR-DRIVE SYSTEM

A fan is mounted in a duct running from the upper storage system to the lower storage system.

It has a continuously variable range of speed, hence a variable rate of airflow. It is set so as to always provide an airflow of at least 80 cfm, an ample rate to expel old, warm air from the house, to take in cold, fresh air, and to supply air to the greenhouse for plant transpiration.

The fan runs at whatever higher speed is necessary to produce such greater airflow as may be needed to (1) keep the greenhouse warmer than 32°F, or (2) keep the lower storage system amply warm, or (3)—on days that are warm enough and sunny enough so that the rooms may threaten to become too hot—extract enough old air from these rooms and inject enough fresh (colder) air into these rooms so that they will not become too hot.

The fan does not have to provide airflow fast enough to match the solar energy input to the attic during sunny hours because the upper storage system has large thermal capacity and acts as a buffer. The solar input to the upper storage system may extend over a period of six or seven hours only, but the transfer of heat to the lower storage system continues over the full 24-hour period.

The purposes of running the fan at higher than normal speed do *not* include furnishing a prompt supply of heat to the rooms. Even in a long, cloudy spell, the rooms are kept warm enough merely by direct intake of solar radiation and some downward flow of heat from the attic. Almost never is the lower storage system called on to directly and promptly supply significant amounts of heat to the rooms.

The fan produces, in all, a series of thirteen airflows, provided that the house is tightly closed, i.e., the windows, outer doors, attic vents, and greenhouse vents are closed. Under such circumstances the primary airflow, from upper storage system to lower storage system, produces a train of other flows:

- Flow from the upper storage system to the upper region of the lower storage system, to keep the lower-story floor slab at about 70°F.

- Flow from the upper region of the lower storage system to lower region of that system, to keep that lower region at least as warm as 50°F.

- Flow from the lower region of that system to the lower region of the greenhouse. (NOTE: The air that thus enters the greenhouse is at about 50°F and has high (near 100%) relative humidity and a slightly higher-than-normal concentration of CO_2—circumstances that favor plant growth.)

- Flow horizontally across the greenhouse plants. On cold winter nights the airflow warms the plants. (In summer it cools them.)

- Flow from the greenhouse into the exhaust duct.

- Flow within this duct, which serves as a key portion of an air-to-air heat exchanger.

- Flow from this duct to the outdoors.

- Inflow of fresh air via a larger cross-section duct that serves as the other key portion of the air-to-air heat exchanger.

- Flow from this duct to an upper-story room that always has an open passage to the stairwell.

- Flow (by gravity convection) of the newly introduced air (which is slightly colder and more dense than typical air in the rooms) down the staircase to the lower rooms.

- Return flow of warmer, lower-story air to the upper story via the stairwell.

- Flow of upper-story air upward, via grilles, into the lower (cooler) region of the upper storage system (attic).

- Upward flow of air in the attic. (The air picks up heat not only from the water-filled containers but also from such portions of the wooden trusses as receive solar radiation. By the time the air reaches the upper part of the attic, the air has become very hot.)

The cycle then repeats: air from the upper part of the attic is forced downward into the lower storage system by the fan.

NOTE: For an account of changes made in the fan system in 1983, see chapter 9.

OTHER SPECIAL SYSTEMS

The duct that carries fresh air into the house is arranged to be coaxial with and to enclose the duct that carries old greenhouse air to the outdoors so that the incoming air will pick up some heat from the outgoing air. In this way some air-to-air heat exchange results. (To provide a high-efficiency exchanger would not be cost-effective: the outgoing greenhouse air, often as cold as 45° or 55°F, contains little heat.)

The living-area south walls are integrated with the greenhouse optically (for daylighting and for a broad view to the south) but partially *isolated* from the greenhouse thermally. Thus at all times the room occupants command a broad view through the full-width south windows and through the greenhouse's south and roof glazing, yet room temperature is little affected even when the greenhouse becomes as cold as 35° or as hot as 85°.

A large fraction of south window area in the living region acts as a thermosyphoning air collector. This system uses two sheets of widely spaced glass and, midway between them, a sheet of semitransparent, semiabsorbant plastic. Solar radiation is absorbed by this sheet and warms it; the sheet heats the air in the adjacent thick airspaces; and the warm air rises by thermosyphon into the upper storage system (attic).

Nearly every room (other than bathrooms) has windows on two adjoining sides for bilateral daylighting. Every window has an area of about 7 sq. ft. or more.

Every room (other than bathrooms) has enough windows and/or doorways to allow ample cross drafts in summer. Every east, west, and north window is fully openable.

The east, west, and north windows, when closed, are tightly sealed, moderately reduce glare, have high solar transmittance, and provide fairly high thermal resistance (of the order of R-4 or R-5).

NONSPECIAL SYSTEMS

The walls and north roof are insulated extremely well—far better than was customary in the solar-heated houses of ten years ago. For a 6,500 degree day (DD) location one should use a true R-30 to R-50 or thereabouts. (Warning: When the nominal R-value is 30, for example, the true value may be only 15 or 20 if small gaps have been left in the insulation. If there is some circulation of air within the walls, and especially if there is some infiltration, small gaps can be seriously harmful. Nearly all builders leave gaps in the insulation. Many do not know how to avoid doing so; others know but are unwilling to take the time to do the job right.)

The foundation walls are insulated on

the exterior faces. Adequate drainage is provided so that no water can back up between the insulation and the walls.

An extremely tight and durable vapor barrier is provided, such as a 0.006-in. polyethylene sheet, to (a) prevent moist room air from penetrating into the insulation and producing condensation, thus degrading the performance of the insulation; and (b) prevent infiltration.

To insure that the vapor barriers on the east, west, and north walls are not punctured where the upper-level floor meets these walls, that floor does *not* meet those walls. An extra inner set of studs supports that floor, thus the lower half of the house has two nearly independent sets of walls.

Chapter 5

ATTIC SOLAR WINDOW

The most important (and most remark-able) component of the Shrewsbury House solar heating system is the attic solar window.

Because it employs a set of louvers that somewhat correspond (in size, spacing, and slope) to the treads of a staircase, this window has been called by its inventor a *Solar Staircase*™. The name is certainly apt, and it has been trademarked. The window system as a whole has been patented. (See the appendix.)

DESIGN GOALS

The attic solar window is intended to be:

   large—should occupy a very large fraction of the south roof area, so that a very large amount of solar energy can be collected;

   highly transmissive of solar radiation in winter;

   low-transmissive in summer;

   capable of performing as a typical roof to exclude rain, snow, and wind;

   resistive to heat flow—R-value to be about 6 or greater;

   entirely passive—no moving parts, nothing to adjust;

   durable, despite prolonged exposure to temperatures as high as 140° or 150°F;

   inexpensive—to cost no more than about twice as much as a convention-al shingled and insulated roof.

PRINCIPLE OF DESIGN

The attic solar window includes many transparent sheets and many airspaces.

Together these provide an R-value of about 6.

The window includes a set of reflective louvers that are nearly horizontal. They allow the sun's rays to pass through relatively freely at midday in winter, i.e., when the sun's rays make an angle of less than 45° with the horizontal plane. But at midday in summer, when the sun's rays make angles far exceeding 45° with the horizontal, the louvers reflect nearly all of the direct radiation back up to the sky. (Before or after midday, the angle that counts, obviously, is the angle from horizontal of the projection of the sun's rays onto a vertical north-south plane.)

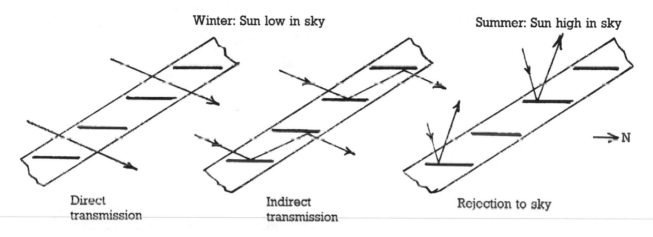

Winter: Sun low in sky   Summer: Sun high in sky

Direct transmission   Indirect transmission   Rejection to sky

Simplified vertical cross section (looking west) of a portion of the south roof, showing the reflective louvers. In midwinter, much direct radiation enters, with no reflection or two reflections. In summer, most of the direct radiation is reflected back to the sky.

The widths, spacings, and slopes of the louvers and the number of glazing sheets used are carefully chosen to be appropriate to the latitude of the house, the steepness of the roof, and the water storage system specifications (total amount of water used, locations of the water-filled carboys, and desired temperature of the water.)

Close above the set of louvers is a glazing sheet of tempered glass. Being glass, it absorbs most of the ultraviolet component of the incident solar radiation; it transmits practically none of the harmful UV radiation that is capable of degrading plastic sheets. Being tempered, it is strong and tough; it can withstand high winds, large snow loads, and hailstones. It is entirely waterproof and windproof. It is extremely durable.

Close below the set of louvers is a set of spaced sheets of transparent plastic of especially durable type. These add greatly to the R-value of the window—without adding greatly to the weight or cost.

All of the components are fixed. None moves, none requires adjustment.

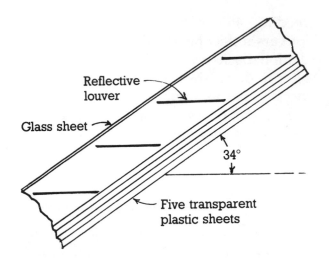

A more complete cross section of a portion of the south roof, looking west. Note that the reflective louvers are situated between the glass sheet and the set of five transparent plastic sheets.

The reflective louvers play an additional helpful role concerning the fraction of the low-angle solar radiation that, on striking the set of plastic sheets, is reflected by those sheets. The reflected radiation is reflected steeply upward and most of it strikes a reflective louver situated close above and is reflected steeply downward by it to-ward the attic interior. (See the diagram.) Thus most of the radiation that is reflected by the set of plastic sheets "on first try" returns for a second try—and most of it then succeeds in entering the attic. I understand that the overall transmittance of the attic solar window with respect to midwinter direct radiation is considerably increased by this recovery, or salvage, process; without this recovery, the transmittance would be about 50%; with it, the transmittance is about 70%.

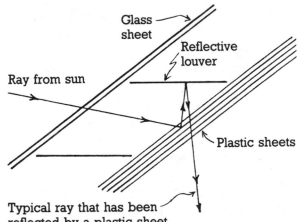

Typical ray that has been reflected by a plastic sheet and then by a reflective louver and ultimately enters the attic

DETAILED DESIGN

The slope of the south roof of the Shrewsbury House is 8 on 12. That is, the roof makes an angle of arctan $8/12$, or about 34°, with the horizontal.

The overall dimensions of this roof (not including the greenhouse roof) are 37 ft. × 18 ft.

The gross area of the glazing on this roof is about 540 sq. ft. (32 ft. × 17 ft.).

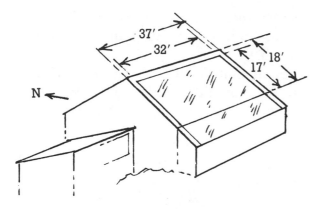

Dimensions of south roof of attic and of the attic solar window.

To describe this solar window in detail, one must describe the glass sheets, the set of louvers, the set of transparent plastic sheets, the supporting trusses, and the assembly means.

Glass Sheets

The glass sheets are 76 in. × 46 in. × $\frac{3}{16}$ in. and are tempered. They are standard sheets such as are manufactured for use as patio doors. Thus they are inexpensive when bought in large quantity.

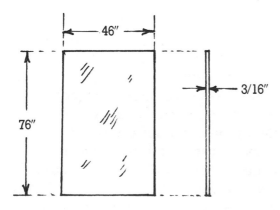

Dimensions of a typical sheet of glass for attic solar window.

Set of Louvers

Each louver, or tread, consists of a shiny aluminum film protected on both faces with a thin layer of tough plastic.

The louver is 4 in. wide and about 4 ft. long. It runs east and west and is nearly horizontal, sloping about 3° upward toward the south.

Each louver is about 3 in. higher up than the next one below it. Thus (when applied to an 8-on-12 roof) the south edge of each louver is approximately directly above the north edge of the next louver below it.

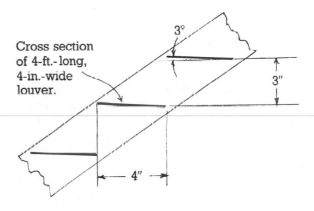

Cross section of 4-ft.-long, 4-in.-wide louver.

Cross section of a portion of the attic solar window, looking west, highly simplified. Shows the tilt, spacing, etc., of three of the louvers.

The individual louver, about 4 ft. long, sags about ¼ in. at the center. Such sag may actually be helpful in winter—it may slightly increase the amount of (twice reflected) radiation that proceeds into the attic proper without striking (and being partially absorbed by) the adjacent wooden members discussed in a later paragraph (the main upper members of the trusses).

NOTE: By midwinter of 1983, the aluminum-film louvers had developed sag and also some twist, which impaired the performance appreciably. The decision was then made that, in the future, such films should be replaced by back-to-back strips of low-cost silvered glass. The glass strips cost considerably more than the aluminum films, but have, over a period of many years' use, a considerably higher reflectivity, which would result in improved thermal performance and would make it permissible to use a somewhat smaller, less costly, attic solar window. They should have a useful life, exceeding 20 years.

Set of Transparent Plastic Sheets

The set includes five sheets, all parallel to one another and to the glass sheets described above. Between successive plastic sheets are ¾-in. airspaces. The set of five sheets is situated close below the set of louvers.

The sheets are of 0.005-in. polyester (mylar). Such a sheet has high transmittance (about 90% for solar radiation, including the visual and near-infrared components). Yet it has high (about 90%) absorptance for the far-infrared radiation such as is emitted by objects that are at about 50° to 150°. Thus such a sheet is virtually equivalent—regarding stopping convection and blocking far-infrared radiation—to a typical sheet of glass. The mylar sheet is highly resistant to solar radiation from which the UV component has been excluded. The material is fully transparent (not merely translucent), very tough, and very durable. It is easily cut with scissors or a

sharp knife. (It is also flammable and burns rapidly if you ignite it with a match.)

Such material costs about $0.35 per sq. ft. in small quantities (in 1983), and somewhat less in large quantities.

Supporting Trusses

Within the solar attic is a set of special trusses. Each is of wood and is 29 ft. long. The trusses lie in vertical planes and run north and south. They are 4 ft. apart on centers.

They serve many purposes, including holding up the roof and the attic floor. (The attic floor does not rest on the partition walls. The entire load is borne by the perimeter walls. Each end of each truss rests on the main south wall of the house or the main north wall.)

The design of the cross-brace system of the trusses is such that clear walkways exist.

Assembly

The trusses, 4 ft. apart on centers, are mounted on the north and south perimeter walls.

The glass sheets (46 in. wide) are mounted 4 ft. (48 in.) apart on centers. Thus there are 2-in. intervals between adjacent sheets.

The glass sheets rest on butyl rubber strips that rest, in turn, on the upper sloping members of the trusses.

Above the location where two glass sheets are adjacent to one another is a pine 2 × 4; it too is provided with butyl rubber strips. The 2 × 4 presses downward, slightly compressing the butyl strips above and below the glass sheets,

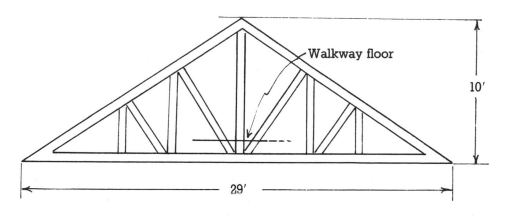

A truss. Schematic, not to scale.

thus providing airtight and watertight seals above and below these sheets.

Above the 2 × 4, and pressing downward on it, is an aluminum cap strip. In cross section, it is slightly wider than the 2 × 4 and nearly as deep. Thus it almost entirely shields the 2 × 4 from the sun's rays.

Flat-head steel screws secure the 2 × 4 to the truss member.

Between each glass sheet and the next one down the slope from it there is a ½-in. gap filled with an elastic, long-life, silicone caulking compound.

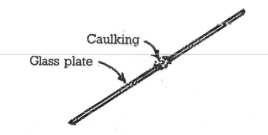

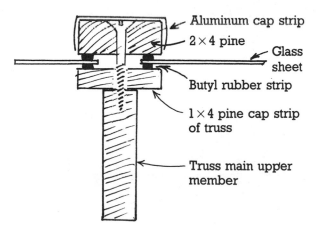

Cross section of portions of two adjacent glass sheets showing details of support system. Not to scale.

The reflective treads (louvers) are mounted within frames of fir wood. The assemblies are prepared elsewhere, e.g., in a workshop, or in the garage of the house in question.

The frame length and width match the length and width of the individual sheet of glass. The frame depth is 4 in. The frame itself is made, and the 4-ft.-long treads are then installed in it. The ends of each tread may be secured by staples, cement, or an anchoring block.

The frame longitudinals are notched at the end to accommodate the east-west purlins of the roof system.

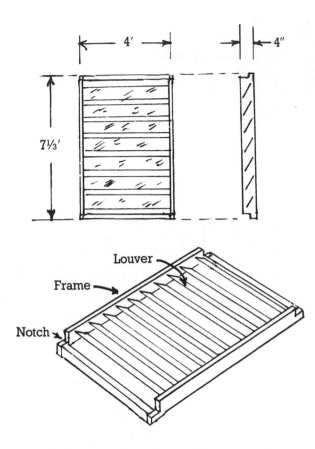

Schematic drawings of frame and
louvers. Not to scale.

Fir wood is chosen because it with-
stands sunlight and high temperatures
well. Unlike the pine 2×4s situated
above the glass sheets, the frames are
exposed to much sunlight and to temperatures as high as 140° or 150°F.

The five transparent mylar sheets are
cut to match the size of the frames, and
are then spaced and secured by means
of junior frames—frames that are only
¾ in. thick.

These frames also are made of fir.
Each strip is rectangular (¾ in. × ¾ in.)
in cross section.

Each mylar sheet is attached to a junior frame with adhesive tape, then the

assembled junior frames are attached to
one another and to the large frame
holding the louvers.

These grand assemblies are then installed between adjacent trusses.

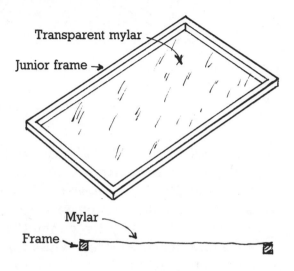

Various views of junior frame with
transparent mylar sheet attached to it.

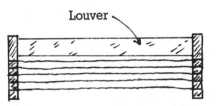

Cross section of five junior frames,
with transparent mylar sheets, joined
to the frame that supports the louvers.

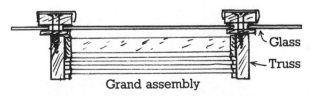

Cross section of portion of solar window,
looking downward toward the south.
Schematic only, not to scale.

TRANSMITTANCE*

Because the attic solar window is sloping and includes a staircaselike set of reflective louvers, its transmittance is not a single number but a large set of numbers. Different values apply to different directions of the sun, times of day, and times of year. This is especially true with respect to direct radiation, but applies also (to a lesser extent) to diffuse radiation, inasmuch as diffuse radiation tends to be most intense from sky regions close to the direction of the sun (except on very heavily overcast days). In upshot, when one asks, "What is the transmittance of the attic solar window?" one must expect different answers for each type of radiation (direct and diffuse), different times of day, and different times of year.

Transmittance on sunny December 21 At noon the transmittance of *direct* radiation is about 70%, and the value pertinent to the daytime as a whole is not far from 70%. For the daytime as a whole the transmittance of *diffuse* radiation from the entire hemisphere of sky is about 40%. Of course, a much higher value, such as 70%, applies to diffuse radiation coming just from the lower half of the south sky in the quadrant between southwest and southeast.

Transmittance on overcast December 21 Here one is concerned with *diffuse* radiation only, and the transmittance with respect to such radiation is about 40%.

Transmittance on sunny June 21 At noon, the transmittance of *direct* solar radiation is very low, about 23%. For the daytime as a whole the transmittance is about 7%. This figure is far below the 23% figure because, at off noon times of this day, the sun is more northerly; its rays are less capable, or entirely incapable, of penetrating the set of louvers. As is well known, the sun rises on this day north of east and sets north of west. With respect to *diffuse* radiation throughout a sunny June 21, the transmittance is about 25%.

Transmittance on sunny April 15 and sunny August 28 On these two dates, each about 36 days from the June 21 solstice, the transmittance with respect to *direct* radiation, for the daytime as a whole, is about 15%.

* The transmittance values presented here must be regarded as provisional and approximate only, as explained in a note on page 75.

OTHER PROPERTIES

Area of attic solar window:

The gross area is 32 ft. × 17 ft. = 544 sq. ft.

The net area is 90% of this, i.e., about 485 sq. ft.

Thermal resistance of attic solar window:

The resistance is R-6, i.e., 6 [ft.^{2} hr. °F/Btu].

Chapter 6

UPPER THERMAL-STORAGE SYSTEM

The Shrewsbury House includes two formal thermal-storage systems: the upper thermal-storage system, in the attic, and the lower thermal-storage system, beneath the lower story. Here we discuss just the former, which is in many ways the more interesting and the more important of the two.

DESIGN GOALS

The upper storage system is intended to be situated close below the attic solar window, so that solar radiation may be received directly.

It employs transparent containers, so that: (a) solar energy may penetrate directly into the container contents (water) and a significant fraction of the radiation entering the container will be absorbed there; and (b) much of the visual-range component of the solar radiation will escape prompt absorption and accordingly provide a high level of illumination in the attic. Thus it may contribute to the illumination of the rooms immediately below, as explained in a later section. (This latter consideration—daylighting the rooms—is obviously a minor one if, as is here the case, the rooms in question have several large windows.)

Other goals and intentions are indicated in chapter 4.

DETAILED DESIGN

A total of about 18,000 lb. of water is used—about 9 tons.

Ordinary water absorbs, in a path length of the order of one foot, a negligible amount of the visual-range portion of solar radiation but absorbs a large fraction of the near-infrared portion. If the water contains various common impurities, it may absorb a significant fraction of the visual-range portion also.

No additives have been used: nothing to prevent freezing, control pH, inhibit corrosion, or inhibit the growth of algae.

The containers consist of glass carboys of 6-gal. capacity. Many of these were secondhand, having been used previously for shipment and storage of liquid chemicals. The price of secondhand carboys may be only a small fraction of the retail price (about $8) of new ones bought one at a time. (Initially, some cylindrical plastic containers were used instead of carboys. Recently, the plastic containers have been replaced by 13 gal. glass carboys.)

Each container is loosely capped. Addition of more water (to replace evaporated water) may be necessary in 5 or 10 years.

6-gal. water-filled glass carboy.

The containers were set on the attic floor, with spaces of 1 to 8 in. between them. The total number of containers is about 400. (The attic floor itself consists of 2 × 4s on edge, 8 in. on centers, with a few boards resting on these as a walkway.)

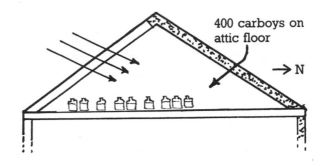

Diagram showing the locations of the carboys on the attic floor.

Insulation

The carboys themselves are not insulated. The only pertinent insulation is that of the attic periphery itself:

- Attic solar window: R-6, as explained in the preceding chapter.

- Attic north roof: R-45 (12 in. fiberglass, 1 in. Thermax).

- East and west gables: R-45. (Vent covers are insulated with 3 in. of Thermax, giving about R-24.)

- Attic floor: Nominal R-11 (3 in. fiberglass), but resistance is hard to estimate in view of many complications, e.g., temperature stratification below, within, and above the attic floor, some radiant flow through the floor as explained elsewhere, and some infiltration upward through the floor.

NOTE: Concerning the validity of the R-values stated here, the attic is as hot as 90° to 130°F in winter and approximately the same is true in summer. The R-values of typical insulating materials tend to be considerably less at temperatures such as these, relative to the values pertinent to 30° or 70°F, for example. Note, however, that the outermost regions of the insulation are typically much cooler than the innermost regions.

Heat-Transfer Area

A typical carboy has a surface of about 5 sq. ft. Accordingly, the total heat-transfer area of the set of carboys is of the order of 2,000 sq. ft.

Expected Temperatures

It was expected that the temperature (say, at the midpoint of the attic region) would be about 85° to 120°F in winter. In summer the temperature may be slightly higher—it may reach, say,

130°F. It is believed that nothing in the attic would be damaged by month-long temperatures as high as 150°F.

Because there is considerable temperature stratification within the water in each carboy and within the attic region as a whole, the temperature at the attic-floor level may be 10° or 20°F lower and the temperature at the attic-peak level may be 10° or 20°F higher than the temperatures mentioned above.

Thermal Capacity

If the 18,000 lb. of water is at about 135°F and cools down to about 80°F, the total quantity of heat given out is about 1,000,000 Btu.

MAIN DUCT

The main duct, which carries air from the upper storage system to the lower storage system, has a rectangular cross section (2 ft. × 2 ft.). The duct runs close to the north sloping roof and to the north wall of the living area. The duct has little insulation.

The fan, described in chapter 9, is situated at the base of the duct.

The duct can be closed off (e.g., in summer) by a damper.

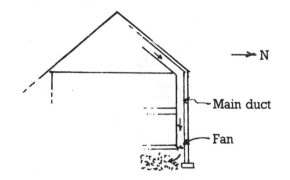

Vertical cross section, looking west, showing the location of the main duct.

Chapter 7

LOWER THERMAL-STORAGE SYSTEM

Indicated in this chapter is the detailed design of the lower thermal-storage system—a bin of stones that extends under the entire area of the lower story.

The design goals have been listed in chapter 4.

DETAILED DESIGN

Stones

The stones are 1 to 2 in. in diameter, with a total mass of about 100 tons. They were washed before being installed.

Containment

The stones, which fill a region 2½ ft. deep, rest directly on the ground; there is no vapor barrier beneath them. They are confined at the sides by the foundation walls, i.e., by the rectangular, 36 ft. × 28 ft. array of vertical concrete foundation walls. The east, west, and north walls are insulated on the outer side with a vertical slab of 2½-in. Styrofoam and an additional underground 2½-in.-thick Styrofoam skirt that slopes downward and outward at an angle of about 30 degrees from the horizontal.

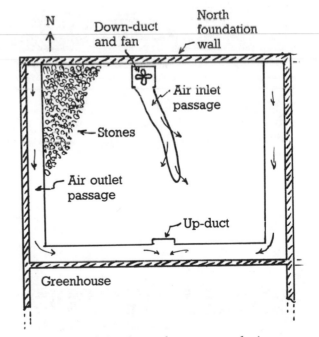

Plan of the bin of stones and air passages beneath the floor of the lower story. Not to scale.

There is no insulation on the foundation wall situated beneath the south vertical windows; no insulation is needed because this wall is flanked by slightly warm greenhouse earth, not cold outdoor earth.

Above the stones, and making contact with them, is the floor of the lower story. This consists of (a) a 4-in. reinforced concrete slab, and below it (b) a 0.006-in. polyethylene vapor barrier, and below it (c) a 1-in. plate of dense fiberglass.

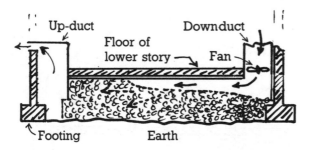

Vertical cross section (looking west) through the centerpoint of the bin of stones. Not to scale.

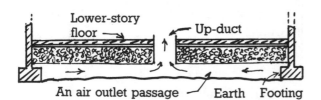

Vertical cross section (looking north) through the up-duct. Not to scale.

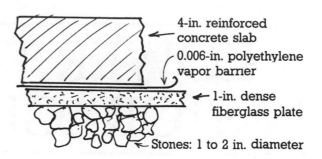

Vertical cross section of a portion of the lower-story floor, with stones beneath.

Air Inlet Plenum

Warm air from the attic enters the bin of stones via an inlet passage that is tongue-shaped and runs generally southward from the north central region of the bin, as indicated in the accompanying diagram. The north end of the passage has a cross-sectional area of about 4 sq. ft., and the passage tapers to nothing at the south end (near the midpoint of the bin). Air flows southward in this passage, and spreads out laterally into the mass of stones.

Air Outlet Plenums

Air emerges from the mass of stones into three outlet plenums, which extend along the lower portions of the east, west, and south foundation walls, i.e., near the footings. Each plenum is 8 in. × 14 in. in cross section. Standard 8 in. × 8 in. × 16 in. concrete blocks form an inner vertical wall and a "roof" for the plenum.

The three passages are, of course, connected, and all of the air they collect flows to an up-duct near the center of the south foundation wall. Here the air flows upward and then southward into the greenhouse, via an 8 ft. × 2½ in. grille beneath the coat closet and door at the north central region of the greenhouse.

Filters

There are two filters in the main airflow: one just upstream from the fan and one between the bin of stones and the greenhouse.

Airflow

To recapitulate: Warm air from the attic is driven by the fan into the air inlet plenum at the top north center of the bin of stones, then flows outward east, west, and south, and slightly downward, where it enters the set of three air outlet plenums that are close to the east, west, and south footings of the house proper. This air then flows upward, in an up-duct, to a slender grille beneath the south door and coat closet, into the lowest part of the greenhouse region, i.e., close to the greenhouse earth.

Details concerning rate of airflow are presented in chapter 9.

TEMPERATURE STRATIFICATION

The upper portion of the bin of stones tends to be warmer than the lower portion. Thus heat may be imparted to the lower-story floor by stones and air at 70° to 80°F, whereas heat may be imparted to the greenhouse by air that is at 50° to 65°F.

Creation of such helpful stratification is facilitated by the slantwise *downward* direction of airflow within the bin of stones. When the air is hottest, i.e., immediately on entering the bin, it is in the upper region of the bin. When the air is coldest, i.e., after having traveled a long distance within the bin and given up much heat to it, it is in the lower region of the bin and soon enters the outlet passages and flows into the greenhouse.

AMOUNT OF HEAT STORED

With a mass of 100 tons (200,000 lb.) and a specific heat of about 0.18 Btu/(lb.,°F), the bin of stones gives out about 36,000 Btu per degree drop in temperature. If a 10° drop occurred, the amount of heat given out would be 360,000 Btu.

Of course, different parts of the bin are ordinarily at different temperatures, and the temperature changes occurring in different parts of the bin differ in magnitude.

There is also much storage of heat in the adjacent foundation walls, in the earth beneath the bin, and in the floor above the bin. However, the heat flows there are slow.

PRESSURE DROP

The bin of stones has such a large aggregate air-pathways cross section—of the order of 50 sq. ft.—that even when the rate of airflow is a maximum (1,500 cfm), the pressure drop is less than 0.1 in. of water. When the rate of airflow has the minimum value—80 cfm—the pressure drop is less than 0.001 in. of water. (Actually, the dynamic pressure head is less than the thermal head, implying that an appreciable amount of helpful thermal stratification occurs.)

EVAPORATION OF WATER

Much water is evaporated from the earth beneath the bin of stones. There is no vapor barrier here, and the forced flow of air entering the bin of stones has low to moderate relative humidity. The evaporation cools the air. The increase in humidity of the air is helpful to the plants in the greenhouse.

Chapter 8

GREENHOUSE

The design goals pertinent to the green-house have been discussed in chapter 4.

The actual design is discussed here.

DETAILED DESIGN

General

The gross dimensions of the green-house area are 37 ft. × 7 ft. However, the 6½-ft.-long west portion is preempted by the entrance vestibule, and a small north central region by a small coat closet that opens to the living region of the house—just its back is visible in the greenhouse. Some space is taken up by a walkway extending the full length of the greenhouse—from the main entrance door at the west to the less-used door at the east. About half the area of the greenhouse is actually available for growing plants.

The grade, or level, of the green-house earth is about 3 ft. higher than that of the lower-story floor. From the greenhouse one descends five steps to reach that floor, or ascends eight steps to reach the second-story floor.

Earth

The greenhouse loam is 5 ft. deep and rests directly on subsoil. Watering is seldom necessary.

Foundation Walls

There are foundation walls on all four sides of the greenhouse. The internal foundation wall—the one between the greenhouse earth and the lower portions of lower rooms—is not insulated. The others are insulated, e.g., by a sloping, underground, 2-in. Styrofoam skirt.

The south foundation wall extends 1½ ft. above the outdoor grade, and this exposed area of that wall is served by transparent insulation—which helps its performance as a Morse (Trombe) wall. The insulation includes an outer sheet of 0.060-in. Kalwall Sun-Lite (polyester and fiberglass) and an inner sheet of duPont Teflon. Strips of ½-in.-thick, dense fiberglass maintain ½-in. airspaces between these two sheets and the foundation wall.

Because the south foundation wall receives much solar energy, is insulated below ground on the south with a Styrofoam skirt, and is flanked by warm greenhouse earth on the north, the lower part of this foundation wall is always

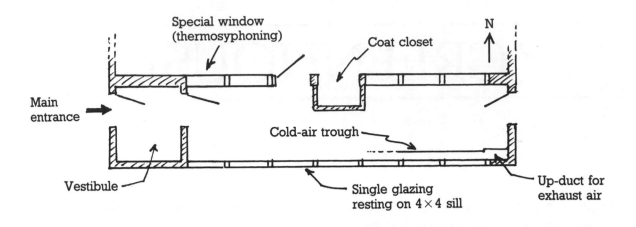

Plan view of greenhouse showing locations of windows and trough for collecting cold air.

above 32°F and the same applies to the earth close to the south and the north. Accordingly, there is no need to extend this foundation as deep as would normally be required.

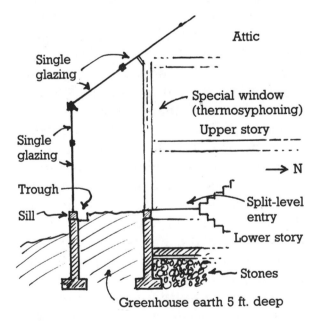

Vertical cross section of the greenhouse (looking west) showing locations of the windows and trough.

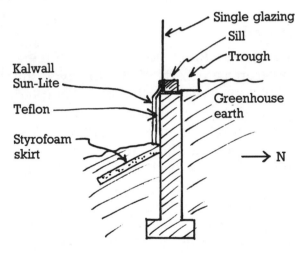

Vertical cross section of the south foundation wall of the greenhouse.

Glass

The lower portion of the greenhouse south face is single-glazed with $3/16$-in. tempered glass, and the same applies to the greenhouse sloping roof. Each glass sheet is 76 in. × 46 in.

The upper portion of the greenhouse south face is single-glazed with double-strength float glass. (The size—46 in. ×3 ft.—is nonstandard, and obtaining tempered sheets of this size would have been difficult and costly.) In any event, there is no need for the glass here to be of the tempered type.

The joints are secured with fir strips and made tight with silicone caulking.

Tempering-Air Inlet

Tempering air enters the greenhouse via an 8-ft.-long, 2½-in.-high grille situated beneath the coat closet and the doorway adjacent to it. As explained in a previous chapter, the tempering air comes from an up-duct associated with the bin of stones.

Typically, the temperature of the tempering air is 50° to 60°F, which is warm enough to prevent the greenhouse from cooling down to 32°F at night.

During the day the greenhouse does not need heat from such an airstream: direct-gain solar energy suffices. The airstream serves, at such times, to reduce any threat of overheating.

Cold-Air Outlet

The coldest air in the greenhouse (air descending along the vertical glazing) descends toward the horizontal trough that flanks the sill and is then guided (more or less) by this trough toward the exhaust duct's intake end, which is at floor level at the east end of the greenhouse. The lowest air in the greenhouse is the coldest air, and this dense air has no option other than to find its way to this duct (which is 8 in. in diameter, except for an initial rectangular cross-section segment).

The duct runs straight upward, then obliquely upward and northward along the slope of the greenhouse roof and the slope of the attic roof. It terminates in an 8-in.-diameter pipe that extends 4 ft. above the peak of the roof and is topped by a turbine. The old greenhouse air (usually moist and, at night, usually cold) emerges via this turbine to the outdoors. Wind turns the turbine and the turbine rotation speeds the airflow.

Vents

At each end of the greenhouse, well above head level, is a vent. Each vent is triangular and has an area of 12 sq. ft. The vent cover is hinged along its vertical (north) edge, and can open wide. It is insulated with Thermax. The open area is protected at all times by a fixed louvered grille and an insect screen.

The vents are opened and closed manually. The original intent was to provide automatic control consisting of passive thermally powered actuators; but because experience has shown that opening and closing the vents once a year (early spring, late fall) may suffice, the plan to provide automatic control was dropped.

When both vents are open, the prevailing west wind can produce a strong flow of air through the greenhouse.

Nighttime Illumination

Electric lights are included in the greenhouse, and when they are turned on at night, they make it difficult for persons standing some distance to the south of the house to see into the living rooms. In other words, they improve the privacy of persons in the house proper.

PROPERTIES

Transmittance of the window The greenhouse south glazing (single glazing) has a transmittance (with respect to solar radiation) of about 88%. The same applies to the glazing of the greenhouse roof.

Area of the window The gross area of the greenhouse window glazing is:

vertical face: 28 ft. × 10 ft.   = 280 sq. ft.

sloping face: 32 ft. × 8½ ft. = 270 sq. ft.

Total   = 550 sq. ft.

The net area is about 85% of this, or about 480 sq. ft.

R-value of the window The R-value is about 1—except if condensation forms.

Thermal storage The greenhouse earth stores much energy. If, in a short period, such as 24 hours, only the uppermost 5 or 10 inches of earth changes temperature significantly, and if one may assume that the uppermost 4 inches changes uniformly and the underlying earth changes not at all, then the thermal capacity is:

(⅓ ft.)(7 ft.)(36 ft.)(100 lb. per ft.^{3} of moist earth) × (0.4 Btu per lb. of moist earth per °F) = 3,400 Btu/°F

The upper part of the south foundation wall also stores much heat, about 2,500 Btu/°F.

Of course, the heat stored in the 100-ton bin of stones plays an important role also—contributing much near-50° air to the greenhouse when the outdoor temperature is very low and the greenhouse threatens to become too cold. Latent heat plays a contributing role here: the air in the lowest part of the bin picks up some moisture from the earth by evaporation, and when this air later comes in contact with the cold glass of the greenhouse, some condensation—and liberation of latent heat—occurs.

Ordinarily, no greenhouse air flows into the living rooms. No duct, no fan, no sliding glass panels are provided for facilitating flow of greenhouse air into the house proper. Such flow would usually do more harm than good, inasmuch as the rooms are already at the desired temperature and humidity. Thus the flow of greenhouse air is generally to the outdoors only. Of course, the house occupants may, at any time, leave open the door between the greenhouse and the central hallway of the living region to allow a flow of air from the greenhouse to the living area. (Such flow is to some extent *forced* if that door is left open and all external doors and all windows are closed. The operation of the fan tends to depressurize the house proper and draw greenhouse air into the house via the open doorway.) Under some circumstances such a flow could improve the temperature or humidity of the living area.

Chapter 9

AIR-DRIVE SYSTEM

The air-drive system is one of the most important features of the house. It performs so many functions, and provides so many airflows (listed in chapter 4), that it deserves much attention.

DETAILED DESIGN

The main components of the air-drive system are a fan, many ducts, and a control system. The scheme described in detail below is the scheme used during the first winter. For changes made during the second winter, see the end of this chapter.

Fan

An ordinary axial-flow, 18-in. diameter, ¼-HP fan is used. It is situated near floor level, close to the center of the north edge of the lower story, at the base of the main down-duct. When operated at full power, it consumes about 300 watts.

Air Path to Outdoors

The fan drives air into and through the bin of stones, and thence into passages that run close to the footings of the east, west, and south foundation walls of the house proper.

Near the center of the passage along the south footing the air enters a 5-ft.-

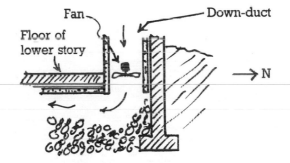

Vertical cross section, looking west. Not to scale.

long up-duct, then turns southward and emerges into the base of the greenhouse space via an 8 ft. × 2½ in. grille beneath the coat closet and doorway adjacent thereto.

The air either (1) remains near the base of the greenhouse, if this air is colder than typical air in the greenhouse (e.g., on a sunny day), or (2) moves toward the top of the greenhouse if the air there is especially cold (e.g., on a cold night).

Air in the south lower portion of the greenhouse eventually flows to the east and enters the exhaust duct. It enters the rectangular entrance to the duct (at floor level, at the east end of the trough discussed elsewhere), flows upward in the duct, then flows slantwise upward and northward toward the peak of the roof in an 8-in-diameter duct, then flows vertically upward in an 8-in.-diameter, 4-ft.-high stack, and emerges, through a turbine, to the outdoors. A strong wind will turn this turbine and help pull the air out of the exhaust duct, i.e., speed up the airflow.

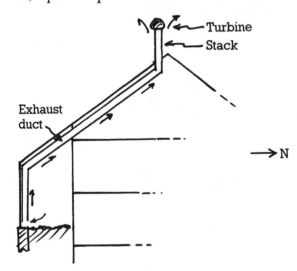

Vertical cross section, looking west, showing the path of the exhaust duct from the lower southeast portion of the greenhouse to the outdoors via a stack and turbine. Schematic only.

Path of Incoming Fresh Air

Fresh air can enter the house near the peak of the attic, via either the west or east gable. In each of these gables is a louvered and screened intake opening.

A long, straight horizontal duct, with a rectangular cross section $14\frac{1}{2} \times 3\frac{1}{2}$ in., runs from the west gable to the east gable. At this latter location fresh air from either gable (or from both) turns and enters a rectangular duct (22 in. $\times$ 8 in.) that runs slantwise downward and southward, then turns and discharges air via a rectangular 24 in. $\times$ 12 in. grille into the southeast upper room.

From here, the air may (1) flow upward into the attic via a ceiling grille, or (2) travel laterally into other rooms and eventually flow upward into the attic via ceiling grilles in either or both of the north upper rooms. Usually the air flowing laterally from the southeast upper room is slightly colder than the air in the lower rooms, and accordingly tends to flow downward into those rooms; after becoming warmed there it rises into the upper rooms and then passes upward into the attic. Thus there is considerable sharing of fresh air among all the rooms of both stories. The fresh air first enters at the southeast upper corner of the living room. The fact that this room has no door insures that, at all times, the fresh air is free to travel toward other parts of the house. Travel from the upper to the lower story, or vice versa, is via the stairwell.

Fresh air can enter via either gable even when the large vent covers are closed by detouring around the covers.

The air-intake entrances in the gables are so designed and so located as to take advantage of the prevailing wind in winter. The wind slightly pressurizes the intake duct and slightly increases the airflow through the entire system.

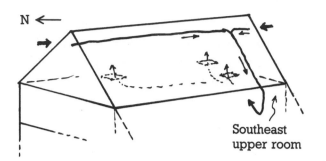

N ←

Southeast
upper room

Schematic diagram showing the intake of fresh air via both gables, the flow of fresh air into the southeast upper room, and the flow to the attic via three grilles in the upper-story ceiling.

Air-to-Air Heat Exchanger

The air-to-air heat exchanger is discussed in chapter 12. It involves the previously mentioned slanting segments of ducts within the attic.

Control System

The power delivered to the fan is normally (i.e., 80% to 90% of the time) about 15 watts. Additional power—between 15 watts and full power (300 watts)—is supplied when the greenhouse threatens to cool down to near 32°F (i.e., on a cold night) or when the living areas threaten to become warmer than 70°F (i.e., during a long, sunny day). The maximum flow rate is 1,500 cfm.

Operating at a 15-watt level, the fan provides an airflow of about 80 cfm, which is ample for insuring an adequate supply of fresh air to the house.

Higher-power operation is subject to proportional control. The control system, of bridge type employing solid-state elements, is situated in a box adjacent to the fan.

Thermistor-type temperature sensors are located (a) in a central region of the house—at the central stairwell, (b) in the lower portion of the greenhouse, and at other locations, e.g., at the top of the bin of stones. During the first winter, however, there was only one sensor controlling fan speed, serving to prevent the rooms from becoming too hot.

PROPERTIES

- Flowrate: 80 to 1500 cfm.

- Power consumption: 15 to 300 watts.

- Expected annual cost of operating the fan (at, say, 10¢/kWh): $70.

- Noise: none, unless you are within a few feet of the fan.

- Attention required of house occupants: none.

- Chilling effect of the indoor moving air: negligible except when the outdoor air is very cold, the rate of intake is high and the people are in the southeast corner of the upper southeast room, where the incoming air enters. Being colder than room air, it settles to the floor and flows horizontally toward the other rooms. However, the incoming air has picked up a little heat (thanks to the heat exchanger) before entering the living area. Thus the chilling effect is minor at worst and, ordinarily, not noticeable. Note that the incoming air is introduced at a *location* where, on sunny days, much direct-gain solar energy is received (upper south room) and at *times* when much solar energy is received when the sun is shining brightly.

CHANGES MADE DURING SECOND WINTER

During the second winter of operation of Shrewsbury House, the air-drive system was changed. The main change was the installation, in the west gable, of a 5-in.-diameter, 22-watt, 100-cfm fan the purpose of which was to deliver outdoor air to the spaces within the east, west, and north walls of the lower and upper stories. This air has very low absolute humidity; consequently, it picks up water molecules from the air in the within–wall airspaces. The overall effect is that the relative humidity in the house is decreased and condensation problems are avoided. (It is now believed that the vapor barrier had not been installed properly—had not been fully sealed. Accordingly, the relative humidity in the rooms had been higher than expected and some condensation had occurred on cold nights on the attic solar window. If the vapor barrier had been properly sealed, moisture problems would not have arisen and there would have been no need to add the extra fan.)

While this 22-watt fan was running, the operation of the main fan was reduced somewhat. Although it often operated at high power on sunny days, it was often off entirely at night. When it was off, the air-to-air heat exchanger discussed in chapter 12 was essentially inoperative.

Operation of the 22-watt fan uses about $10 worth of electrical power per winter.

Chapter 10

SOUTH WINDOW SYSTEM

The south window system is intended to:

- admit much daylight to the south rooms.

- provide wide view from those rooms.

- prevent glare in those rooms (despite the large area of the windows and the lack of any eaves).

- collect much solar energy and deliver this energy—passively, by thermosyphoning—to the attic.

- provide high thermal resistance to heat flow from the south rooms to the greenhouse (at night especially).

- greatly reduce the direct-gain solar energy input to the south rooms in summer.

DETAILED DESIGN

The south window system of the house proper includes eight windows. Five of these are about 13 ft. high, net, and thus serve both stories. Three, above the coat closet and doorway adjacent to it and also near the greenhouse vestibule, are only 6 ft. high. Each window is about 6 in. thick.

The lower edge of a typical window rests on a sill on the south foundation wall of the house proper. The window space is sealed at the bottom.

The uppermost part of a typical window is open to the attic: air is free to flow from the window interior to the attic and vice versa.

Each window has a width of 4 ft. nominal, or about 44 in. clear, and is separated from the next by a built-up post that helps support the attic. Each post is 4 in. wide (in east-west dimension) and is 6 in. deep.

Each window employs three glazing sheets in series. Two are of glass and one is of plastic. The glass sheets are 6 in. apart and the plastic sheet is midway between them. There are no plastic sheets in the lower portions of the windows.

The south glass face of a typical window extends without significant interruption from the sill to the attic, but the north faces of most of the windows are interrupted by the upper-story floor structure. The overall width of the south glass face is about 32 ft., and the same applies to the north face.

The total net solar aperture of the south face is about 290 sq. ft. and the total net solar aperture of the north face is about 240 sq. ft.

A typical glazing sheet consists of tempered glass, 76 in. × 46 in. × 3/16 in. The sheet can easily be removed with a screwdriver. No caulking is used.

A special plastic sheet is situated midway between the glass sheets. It absorbs about 75% of the incident solar radiation, transmits about 20%, and reflects about 5%. This sheet does not extend to the bottom of the window, but stops somewhat short. It is supported mainly from the top, i.e., by a horizontal rod (roller) situated in the extreme south portion of the attic. If it were ever necessary to remove the plastic sheet, for cleaning or replacing, one would first remove the inner (north) glazing sheet.

The lowest two inches of the window space is partitioned off and serves as a

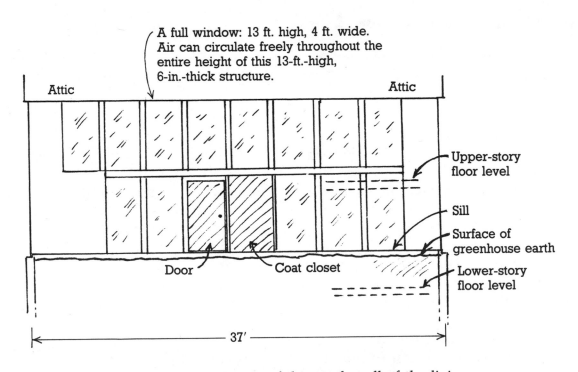

Vertical elevation: full view of the south wall of the living region, looking north, and the south sheets of glass.
(The *lower north* sheets of these windows are less tall, to accommodate the floor structure of the upper story.)

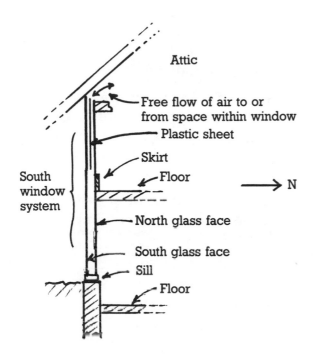

Vertical cross section, looking west, of the south window system. Schematic only.

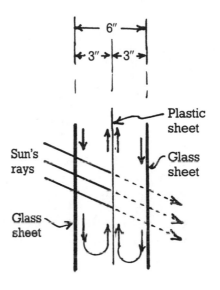

Detail, showing warm air rising close to the plastic sheet and cold air descending close to the two glass sheets.

horizontal pathway, or chase, for electrical wires.

When much solar radiation strikes the plastic sheet, and a fraction of this is absorbed by the sheet, the sheet becomes warm and warms the air that is very close to it (within a fraction of an inch). This warm air rises close to the plastic sheet and flows into the attic, adding to the amount of heat stored there. There are corresponding downward flows of air within the window space; these flows are close to the glass sheets and far (about 2 or 3 inches) from the plastic sheet. Thus the window system as a whole acts as a passive air-thermosyphoning solar collector.

NOTE: The window structure described above has three glazings in series. If these were present independently, each would have a reflectance of about 8%, 5%, and 8% respectively. The actual overall effect is such that when solar radiation strikes the window, about 15% of the radiation is reflected back toward the greenhouse plants. In effect, the reflected radiation simulates the north sky radiation that normally strikes outdoor plants and helps them grow. In summary, the reflected radiation—trapped in the greenhouse—is quite helpful.

PROPERTIES

- Net area of the window: 290 sq. ft. or 240 sq. ft., depending on whether one's attention is focused on the window's south glass or north glass.

- Transmittance of the window: about 20%—low enough to greatly reduce glare as well as direct-gain solar heating in summer.

- Absorptance of the window: about 65%—great enough to permit collection of much solar energy by thermosyphoning.

- Reflectance of the window: about 15%—enough to provide the greenhouse plants with a significant amount of radiation from the north.

- Width of the window area as a whole: the full width of the south face of the house (except for the region near the west end and near the greenhouse vestibule).

- R-value of the window with respect to heat loss at night: estimated to be about 2.8.

NOTE: The intervening plastic sheet actually installed differs sightly from the one specified. Had the specified sheet been used, the R-value would be about 3.2 instead of 2.8.

Chapter 11

NONSOUTH WINDOWS

There are twelve nonsouth windows. In the lower story there are five: three on the north and two on the east. In the upper story there are seven: two on the west, three on the north, and two on the east. Each of these wood-frame windows is about 42 in. × 30 in. Net aperture: 7 sq. ft.

Each window has three glazing layers: two sheets of double-strength float glass 3½ in. apart, and, midway between them, a sheet of special plastic.

The plastic sheet, which has a special coating, transmits a large fraction of the visual component of solar radiation and reflects almost 100% of the middle- and far-infrared, i.e., radiation in the range from 2 to 40 microns and beyond. Thus the transmittance with respect to solar radiation as a whole is about 60% (low enough to be helpful in reducing heat load in summer) while the transmittance of visible light is 75%.

Thanks to the special film and its reflective coating, the R-value of the whole window assembly is about 5. This value applies not only to the glazed area proper but also to the sash frame and the fixed frame.

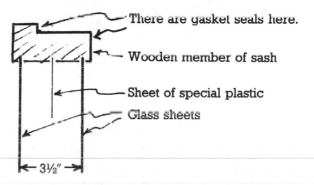

Cross section of a portion of a typical window on the east, west, or north side of the house. (Oversimplified diagram.)

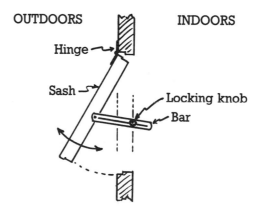

Diagram (schematic only) showing how the window is hinged and how it is held open.

The windows are hinged at the top and can swing open about 3 ft. at the bottom. The window can be held open by rigid bars at each side. Each bar is slotted and engages a fixed (threaded) pin. Each pin has a manually operated locking knob. When the window is fully closed, its bars are nearly vertical, i.e., out of the way.

Two sets of gaskets are provided. The one close to indoors, in first-story windows, prevents in-leak of outdoor air and, in second-story windows, prevents out-leak of indoor air. The one closer to outdoors (for both stories) prevents outdoor air from leaking into the space between sash members and fixed-frame members.

When a window is being closed, the last bit of travel is very positive, being controlled by a special bolt and knob at window-sill level. Thus the gaskets are firmly compressed. Turning the knob to the left releases the window and initiates opening.

The windows can be unhinged and removed, as for cleaning the outer faces.

Comment concerning reducing glare: One of the best ways of reducing glare in a room is to have windows on two sides of the room—bilateral fenestration. In designing typical energy-conserving houses, architects often feel compelled to use very few windows on the east, west, and north sides of the house; in some instances they provide *no* north windows, and consequently some rooms have only one window— one small- or medium-sized window. Result: considerable glare, marginal daylighting, and restricted view. Because the Shrewsbury House nonsouth windows are of high-R type, an ample number of such windows may be provided, and all rooms (except those abutting the garage) have bilateral fenestration. Glare-reduction in the second-story rooms is assisted by the diffuse daylighting from above, i.e., via the light-transmitting ceiling. North room daylighting, more than half of which is from above, sometimes exceeds the level of daylighting in the south rooms.

Chapter 12

OTHER COMPONENTS

CEILING OF UPPER-STORY ROOMS

In each upper-story room, the ceiling is of thin, translucent plastic above which there is a 3-in. layer of special white fiberglass. Above this is a more or less open attic floor: a set of 2×4s on edge (spaced 8 to 12 in. apart on centers) that support the carboys and a walkway.

Accordingly, much of the bright light present in the attic on sunny days is free to flow downward into the upper-story rooms. Thus these rooms are day-lighted not only by their windows but also by the translucent ceilings. The R-value of the ceiling is about R-11.

ATTIC VENTS

At each end of the attic is a pair of triangular vents, for summer use. Each pair is in a gable and is high up, close to the ridge, so that the air that escapes will be the hottest air in the attic.

Each vent is 6½ ft. long and 4½ ft. high and has a nominal area of 14 sq. ft. The effective area is only about 40% as great as this because of the rain-excluding louvers and the insect-excluding screens. The vent covers, insulated with 3 in. of Thermax, have limited space in which to swing, but are hinged in such a way as to allow ample space for airflow and to favor flow close to the peak (the hottest region) of the attic. The total effective vent area at each end of the attic is about 12 sq. ft.

The vents can be opened manually each spring and closed manually each fall. Actually, most are kept closed even in summer, as explained in chapter 13.

WALL INSULATION

A typical portion of an east, north, or west wall includes gypsum board, a vapor barrier (of 0.006-in. polyethylene), 5½ in. of fiberglass, 1 in. of Thermax, and siding. R-value: about 30.

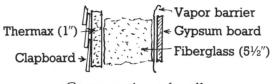

Cross section of wall.

VAPOR BARRIER

On each wall, except the south wall, is a 0.006-in. polyethylene vapor barrier, carefully overlapped and sealed. The barrier runs continuously from the sills of the lower story to the ceiling of the upper story. There is no interruption for the upper-story floor joists: the joists do not touch these walls, but are supported by an independent set of studs. Thus the lower-story walls are about 4 in. thicker than the upper-story walls. All piping and wiring is kept well away from the vapor barrier.

Does the Thermax sheathing constitute a second vapor barrier? Are there, then, two vapor barriers, one near the warm side of the wall and the other near the cold side? Can moisture be-

come trapped between the two?

To some extent the Thermax does indeed serve as a second vapor barrier; more exactly, a barrier to block the flow of moisture and the inflow of cold outdoor air. But there is no threat of moisture becoming trapped between the two barriers, thanks to the negative pressurization of the house. (See the following section.)

A vapor barrier is in place on the warm side of the insulation on the attic gables and attic north roof. (There is a polyethylene sheet beneath the concrete slab of the lower-story floor. It was installed to keep the concrete moist while it was hardening, but now serves no purpose.)

NEGATIVE PRESSURIZATION OF THE HOUSE

Because the fan is at all times expelling air from the house, and because there is very slight pneumatic resistance to the inflow of fresh air via the fresh-air intake duct, the house is at all times under a slight negative pressure.

Accordingly, the direction of leakage of air through a typical region of exterior wall is inward: there is a continual, very small flow of air inward through the house walls. Thus any moisture that finds its way into an exterior wall is likely to be picked up by the very slow inflow of outdoor air—which usually has low absolute humidity (and, as it warms up, very low relative humidity).

The situation in summer is very different, as explained in chapter 13.

AIR-TO-AIR HEAT EXCHANGER

The combination of the exhaust air duct and fresh-air intake duct serves, in effect, as an air-to-air heat exchanger. A 20-ft. length of exhaust duct lies within an equal length of fresh-air intake duct: one contains and embraces the other. Thus some heat in the outgoing air flows through the wall of the inner duct and into the incoming air.

The duct segments in question run

parallel to the south-sloping attic roof, at its east end.

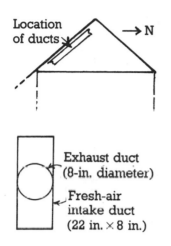

Cross section of ducts.

The accompanying sketch shows the cross sections of the two coaxial ducts— one circular and the other rectangular in cross section.

The heat-exchange efficiency is, of course, low; the area of heat transfer is only about 40 sq. ft. The efficiency ranges from about 10% or 15% when the flow rates are low (of the order of 80 cfm) and only a few percent when the flow rates are high (e.g., 1,500 cfm).

NOTE: It would not be cost-effective to provide a high-efficiency air-to-air heat exchanger, inasmuch as the exhaust air is often as cold as 45° to 55°F. There simply isn't much heat available to be salvaged!

DOMESTIC HOT-WATER SYSTEM

The heart of the hot-water system is an 80-gal. insulated tank situated in the attic. Because the attic is very hot, the tank loses relatively little heat. The tank's final heating is electrical.

Solar preheating is provided in a very simple way. The pipe in which the water flows to this tank is of generous diameter (1¼ in.) and is of a high-conductivity material, copper. One long section of pipe runs horizontally in the upper (hottest) part of the attic, and a preceding section runs horizontally in the lowest (coldest) part of the attic. Water flows first through this lower section, picking up a little heat from the moderately warm air, then flows through the upper section, picking up heat from the very hot air. The water then flows into the tank. The volume of the preheating pipe, which has an over-

all length of 100 ft., is 6 gal. Thus preheating is especially effective if only 6 gal. of water are drawn at one time.

What dollar saving did this DHW solar-preheating system produce during the first year of use? About $300.

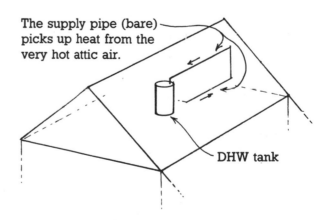

Diagram of DHW solar pre-heating system. Schematic only.

UNDERGROUND AIR-INTAKE DUCT

Beneath the berm on the north side of the house is a large-diameter (24-in.) duct, about 8 ft. long, for admitting outdoor air to the fan chamber and lower storage system. The duct is well screened and barred

The duct is used in summer to bring cooling air to the bin of stones whenever that bin becomes too hot to do its job of keeping the rooms cool. In winter the duct is closed off. The duct is so short that it is not to be regarded as an earth-cooled tube.

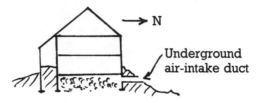

Because this duct is available for intake of outdoor air, it would be possible to leave all windows and outside doors shut all summer and still maintain a comfortable indoor temperature and humidity.

CONTROL OF HUMIDITY AND MOISTURE

The humidity in the house cannot become excessive because of the steady intake of outdoor air (which has low absolute humidity) and the steady expulsion of air from the house to the greenhouse and thence to the outdoors. The outgoing air carries with it the moisture imparted to indoor air by human bodies, cooking activities, showers, etc.

Notice that the heat exchanger, described earlier in this chapter, recovers no moisture. In no way does it impede the ejection of moisture from the house.

Even if the house occupants water the greenhouse plants frequently, there is no threat that the humidity in the living area will become excessive because the greenhouse air flows to the out-

doors only.

The earth beneath the bin of stones plays a helpful role, as far as humidity control is concerned, both in winter and in summer. The roles in these two seasons are opposite. In winter, the dry warm air circulated through the bin of stones picks up moisture from the slightly moist earth, and the added moisture in the air flowing to the greenhouse helps plant growth. In summer, the air circulated through the bin may be too humid, and some of its moisture may be condensed on the cold earth or on the lowest, coldest stones of the bin of stones.

The typical humidity of room air, in winter, is 40% to 50%.

SOLAR-HEATED GARAGE

The 24-ft. × 24-ft., two-car garage is attached to the west side of the house and

is on-grade with the lower story. There is a door between the garage and the northwest room of the lower story.

The double-width, 16½-ft.-wide garage door shuts fairly tightly.

High up on the south side of the garage is a 16-ft.-long, 4-ft.-high window that provides much direct-gain solar heating—as well as illumination for the long workbench immediately below the window. The sloping, white-painted portion of ceiling reflects daylight downward toward the workbench. At night, with the garage's upper south electric lights on, this brightly lighted sloping surface illuminates the area around the main entrance steps to the house with diffuse (nonglare) light.

Cross section of the garage, looking east.

Chapter 13

OPERATION
IN SUMMER

At this time (May 1983) the house has been through one summer. Results exceeded expectations. Some of the available operating procedures listed below were not needed.

OPERATING PROCEDURES AVAILABLE

In summer these operating procedures are available to the house occupants:

- The attic vents can be opened. The extent is determined by two factors: the attic, and thus the upper-story rooms, should not become too hot (and certainly the temperature in the hottest part of the attic should not exceed about 150°F—since higher temperatures might damage some of the materials there); yet a significant amount of preheating of the domestic hot-water supply should still occur.

- Some or all of the openable windows can be opened, as seems appropriate. There are twelve such windows located so as to provide cross drafts. Usually, on very hot days, the windows will be left closed so that the house may remain cool. Often, on cool nights, the windows will be opened. Note, however, that the house occupants have the option of leaving the windows closed—untouched; the rooms should remain at a comfortable temperature (about 70° to 80°F) thanks to the other temperature control features of the house.

- The vents at the ends of the greenhouse can be opened. (Plans called for installing automatic actuators that would open the vents whenever the greenhouse air became hotter than a specified temperature, such as 60°, 70°, or 80°F. However, no such actuators have yet been installed and there appears to be little need for them. Manual operation in spring and fall is simple and effective.) When the vents are open, hot air can escape, and the prevailing wind from the west speeds the escape. Of course, the occupants may also open the greenhouse doors to the outdoors. This further speeds the venting; here too the prevailing wind is very helpful.

- The damper in the tube extending from outdoors (just north of center of north foundation wall) to the fan chamber can be opened so that the fan can bring in outdoor air when that air is cool (e.g., at night). At the same time, the damper in the duct extending from attic to fan chamber can be closed so that no hot attic air will be delivered to the lower storage sys-

tem. Cooling of this storage system may be started in May so that, by the time the hot weather has arrived, the bin of stones will be at about 65°F.

- An access panel in the lower region of the central hallway can be opened to permit the fan to deliver cool air from the lower storage system directly to the central region of the house.

- An access panel adjacent to the fan can be opened, and the fan position slightly changed, so that the fan can deliver cool outdoor air (e.g., at night) directly to the rooms, bypassing the lower storage system.

HELPFUL FEATURES

In summer, only a moderate amount of solar energy enters the attic via the attic solar window. See the following section for an estimate of the amount.

Also, only a moderate amount of solar radiation enters the rooms via the windows. The very large south windows of the south rooms receive little solar radiation because, in summer, the sun is so high and, during many hours of the day, is in the northern hemisphere. Also, these large windows have low transmittance and a moderately high R-value, as explained in chapter 10. They also create a thermosyphoning effect that delivers much of the captured energy to the attic.

The other windows also have only moderately large transmittance, thanks

mainly to the intermediate glazing sheet.

The walls have such high R-value and are so tightly sealed that they transmit little heat.

Little heat flows downward from the upper storage system to the rooms below because of the very helpful thermal stratification within that system.

The concrete slab of the lower-story rooms is very helpful inasmuch as it is (on hot summer days) cooler than the air in those rooms. The slab can remain cool almost indefinitely, thanks to its large thermal mass and the much greater thermal mass of the bin of stones immediately below, provided the bin is cooled off at night several times a week.

Under various circumstances the

house occupants may decide to leave open the door between the greenhouse and the living area. The resulting thermal coupling may be advantageous under some circumstances and certainly may be disadvantageous under other circumstances.

The exhaust-stack turbine, if turned by the wind, helps exhaust hot greenhouse air.

When the attic air is very hot and the gable vents are open, this hot air tends to flow strongly out through the vents, thus encouraging warm air in the rooms to flow upward into the attic; this in turn helps draw cool air into the rooms.

The heat exchanger (discussed in previous chapters) is inoperative, of course, whenever windows of the living area are open, or when the fan is bringing in air via the underground duct on the north side of the house.

If, during a hot and humid day, the occupants arrange for indoor air to be circulated through the bin of stones, and if this bin is cool (as is expected to be the case throughout the summer), some moisture from the air may condense on the cool stones; accordingly, the air that is returned to the rooms from the bin may be relatively cool and dry.

If, while outdoor air is being introduced by the fan via the underground duct, all windows and outside doors are closed, the house will be under positive pressure. Thus there will be a steady tendency for air to migrate slowly *outward* through any small cracks, etc., in the outer walls. Accordingly, any condensate (water droplets, moisture) that is present in those walls in summer will be flushed to the outdoors.

CALCULATION OF SOLAR RADIATION INTAKE BY THE ATTIC

In summer the solar attic takes in very little solar radiation. During a sunny day in June the effective transmittance of the attic solar aperture with respect to direct radiation is about 7%, as explained in chapter 5. With respect to diffuse radiation the transmittance is about 25%.

I estimate that the amount of direct radiation entering the attic via the attic south window on a sunny day in June is

$$[300 \text{ Btu/(hr. ft.}^2)](485 \text{ ft.}^2)(7\%)$$
$$(16 \text{ hr.}) = \text{about } 160,000 \text{ Btu}$$

and the amount of diffuse radiation entering is

$$[30 \text{ Btu/(hr. ft.}^2)](485 \text{ ft.}^2)(0.25)$$
$$(16 \text{ hr.}) = \text{about } 58,000 \text{ Btu}$$

The total, then, is about 220,000 Btu. This is about ⅓ of the energy intake via the attic solar window on a sunny December 21.

Note Added in Galley Proof

Some detailed computer calculations made in November 1982 by N. B. Saunders indicate, I am told, that the problem of computing accurately the transmittance of the south-roof solar aperture with respect to direct radiation and diffuse radiation at different times of the day and different times of the year is a very difficult one. Adding to the difficulties are (1) the reflections from the glass sheets, from the reflective louvers, and from the set of plastic sheets, and (2) various obliquity effects (vignetting). Thus the transmittance data presented here and in chapter 5 must be regarded as approximate only, and main reliance should be placed on the *actual performance* data presented in chapter 14.

Chapter 14

PERFORMANCE

Discussions of goals, strategies, and actual design are now complete. How well does the house perform? The immediately following sections show that it *should* perform well, and the last two sections show that it *does* perform well.

NOMINAL PERFORMANCE IN GENERAL

Typical Sunny Daytime in Winter

During a typical sunny daytime in winter, solar energy pours into the attic via the attic solar aperture, warming the air and the water-filled carboys. It also pours into the greenhouse, warming the greenhouse earth and air; and some pours onto the upward-projecting south foundation wall of the greenhouse, warming this wall. Some pours through the big south windows of the south rooms, warming those rooms by direct radiation, and some is absorbed within those windows and causes this air to rise, by thermosyphoning, into the attic.

The fan runs steadily, transporting hot air from the upper storage system to the lower storage system and forcing an airflow from the latter storage system to the greenhouse and thence, via a special duct (part of a heat exchanger), to the outdoors. The exhaust air is somewhat warm and contains some mois-

ture; thus some heat is lost and some moisture is eliminated.

At the same time, the slight negative pressurization of the house causes an inflow of cold outdoor air via the heat exchanger, and this still fairly cold air enters the upper southeast room, diffuses to the other rooms of both stories, and eventually finds it way into the attic.

All vents, exterior doors, and windows are closed. In particular, the greenhouse vents should be kept closed from about November 1 through May 1, and the greenhouse doors should generally be kept closed from September 1 to July 1. Of course, while a vent or door of the greenhouse is open, little or no air exits via the heat exchanger; accordingly, little or no heat is recovered by it. But fresh air continues to enter the rooms via the exchanger.

The fan automatically speeds up, delivering fresh, cool air to the rooms and slightly warm air to the greenhouse, whenever (1) the rooms tend to become too hot, or (2) the greenhouse threatens to cool down to 32°F.

All of the rooms are at about 70°F, and the humidity is in an acceptable range, not far from 40% relative humidity. There is a steady inflow of fresh air. All rooms have good daylighting, without glare. Everything is silent: there are no moving parts other than the fan (audible only if you are standing within a few feet of it), the greenhouse vent covers, and air.

Typical Cold Night in Winter

The fan continues to run, transporting about 100 cfm of warm air from the upper storage system to the lower storage system, driving cool air (at about 50°F) to the greenhouse, driving greenhouse air to the outdoors, and causing a steady inflow of cold, fresh air to the upper southeast room.

All vents, including those in the greenhouse, and all exterior doors and windows remain closed.

Operation is fully automatic. The fan continues to run at whatever speed the control system judges to be appropriate. There are no thermal shades or shutters for the house occupants to close—there *are* no thermal shades or shutters.

All of the rooms remain at about 70°F. The humidity remains satisfactory.

The greenhouse cools down only very slowly, thanks to the heat stored in the greenhouse earth and greenhouse south foundation wall, and thanks also to the stream of highly humid, slightly warm air (at about 50°F) flowing steadily from the lower storage system to the greenhouse. It is helpful also that the coldest air in the greenhouse—the air descending along the single south glazing—is preferentially collected and ejected.

Of course, the overall excellent insulation of the house helps retain heat, and the greenhouse acts as a buffer region for the big south windows of the living area. The overall airtightness helps also.

Help is provided also by intrinsic heat—heat from the occupants' bodies, from electric light bulbs, from the cooking stove, and from other appliances. Because the house is so well insulated and so airtight, intrinsic heat plays a significant role. Nonetheless, its role is relatively less important than in a superinsulated houe that is very small yet has the same amount of intrinsic heat. The Shrewsbury House, with its floor area of 2,200 sq. ft. (not including greenhouse or garage), does not qualify as very small!

CALCULATIONS CONCERNING THE ATTIC SOLAR WINDOW (R-6)

Here are presented some calculations (rough estimates) of expected performance of the attic solar window.

Sunny December 21

Total intake of solar energy per hour near midday:

By direct radiation: about 250 [Btu/(hr. ft.^{2})](485 ft.^{2})(0.7) or about 85,000 Btu/hr.

By diffuse radiation: about 50 [Btu/(hr. ft.^{2})](485 ft.^{2})(40%) or about 10,000 Btu/hr.

Total: 95,000 Btu/hr., or about 90,000 Btu/hr. after allowing for vignetting.

Amount per sunny December 21 day: about 620,000 Btu.

Heat loss at night If the attic temperature is 120°F and the outdoor temperature is 20°F, the temperature difference is 120°F − 20°F = 100 F degrees. The effective area of the window, regarding heat loss, is the gross area: 550 sq. ft. Thus the heat loss per nighttime hour is:

$$\frac{(100°F)(550 \text{ ft.}^2)}{6[\text{ft.}^2 \text{ hr. } °F/Btu]} = \text{about 9,000 Btu/hr.}$$

The loss per 16-hour night is thus (16)(9,000) = about 145,000 Btu.

Heat loss during the day To compute the heat loss during a sunny day is very difficult because much of the heat lost is heat produced (by solar radiation) *within* the structure of the attic solar window. That is, miscellaneous absorption and reflection processes of the various glazing layers and the adjacent rafters cause the glass and plastic components of the attic solar window to become warm; in fact, estimates indicate that the lowest plastic sheet (the one in di-

rect contact with the hot attic air) is at about the same temperature as the attic air itself. This implies that practically none of the radiant energy that is actually absorbed within the attic is lost via the attic solar window: the losses are made up practically entirely by the amount of solar radiation absorbed by the window components themselves. In summary, the sunny daytime loss is 0 Btu.

Heat loss over 24 hours Combining these estimates, or guesses, one arrives at a figure of 145,000 + 0 = 145,000 Btu per 24 hours, i.e., per one night and sunny day.

Balance (net gain) If the solar intake is through the attic solar window, the attic is at 120°F, and the outdoor temperature is 20°F, then from the results obtained above, the net gain is:

620,000 Btu − 145,000 Btu = 475,000 Btu

Overcast December 21

Here there is no direct radiation. I assume the diffuse radiation is 60% the sunny-day diffuse radiation, i.e., about (60%)[50 Btu/(hr. ft.^{2})](485 ft.^{2}) or 14,500 Btu/hr. About 55% of this is transmitted, i.e., (14,500 Btu/hr.)(.55) = about 8,000 Btu/hr. or about 50,000 Btu per overcast December 21 day.

How does this compare with the heat loss through this same attic solar window? It is closely comparable—if the attic is at 120°F and the outdoor temperature is 20°F, as is made clear on the previous page. The solar intake is 8,000 Btu/hr. The heat loss is about 9,000 Btu per nighttime hour or about 8,000 Btu per cloudy daytime hour (and part of this is made up by absorption of radiant energy by the window itself). Thus during an overcast December 21 daytime, the solar intake by the window roughly equals (offsets) the heat loss through this window.

NOTE: If, in midwinter, there are several overcast days in succession, the attic temperature will decrease and the heat loss likewise will decrease. This fact contributes to the house's ability to remain warm throughout a week-long midwinter overcast period.

CALCULATIONS CONCERNING THE GREENHOUSE

The total glazed area of the greenhouse is about 550 sq. ft. and the net area is about 485 sq. ft. Thus the total intake of solar energy on a sunny day in December is about:

$$(485)(ft.^2)(250\ Btu/ft.^2\ hr.)(0.9)(6\ hr.)$$
$$= about\ 650,000\ Btu$$

About 300,000 Btu of this solar energy passes on into the house's thermosyphoning south windows and/or into the south rooms; about 350,000 Btu remain in the greenhouse.

At night the greenhouse is colder than the house proper; consequently, the greenhouse receives heat via the south windows of the house proper. The amount received is estimated at 120,000 Btu per a 24-hour day. Thus the total receipts from the sun and from the south windows of house proper amount to 350,000 Btu + 120,000 Btu =

470,000 Btu.

The 24-hour loss through the greenhouse glass to the outdoors when the greenhouse is at 60°F and the outdoor temperature is 20°F is about:

$$(60\quad 20)(1/0.9)(485)(24)$$
$$= about\ 520,000\ Btu$$

Losses through the greenhouse end walls are two orders of magnitude less than this—a negligible amount.

The small overall deficit implied by the above figures, i.e., the 520,000 − 470,000 = 50,000 Btu deficit, is, of course, made up by (1) heat supplied by the stream of air from the bin of stones to the greenhouse and (2) heat from the greenhouse earth and greenhouse foundation walls.

Obviously, the greenhouse is warmer during sunny hours and colder during cold nights than assumed here.

CALCULATIONS CONCERNING THE THERMOSYPHONING SOUTH WINDOWS

The window system of the south rooms has a net solar aperture of about 290 sq. ft., as explained in chapter 10. The radi-

ation incident is the radiation that has passed through the greenhouse glazing and thus is about 12% less intense than the outdoor solar radiation. At hours far from noon, the opaque greenhouse gables block much solar radiation that might otherwise have reached the window system.

I assume that, on a sunny day in December, the amount of radiation incident on this window system is:

$$(290 \text{ ft.}^2)(300 \text{ Btu/ft.}^2 \text{ hr.})$$
$$(\text{nonblocking factor of } 0.8)(4.3 \text{ hr.})$$
$$= \text{about } 300,000 \text{ Btu}$$

Much of this is absorbed by the thermosyphoning south windows. The upper windows include, as indicated in chapter 10, an intervening plastic sheet that has an absorptance of about 75%. No such sheet is present adjacent to the south edge of the second-story floor structure, but this structure itself is highly absorbing; no such sheet is present in the lower windows. It is estimated that about 50% of the 300,000 Btu incident is absorbed; that is, about 150,000 Btu are converted to heat within the windows, and nearly all of this flows, in the thermosyphoning air, to the attic.

About 20% of the 300,000 Btu, or 60,000 Btu, enters the lower rooms and helps heat them, and the other 30% (another 90,000 Btu) enters the upper rooms and helps heat them.

Note that the 150,000-Btu contribution to attic heat is about 25% of the attic's *gross* intake of solar energy via the sloping south roof and is about 30% of the attic's *net* gain (gross intake minus 24-hour loss). This is, clearly, a big contribution.

Heat Loss

How much heat is lost through the thermosyphoning window system on a cold night? Not much, because the R-value of the window system is moderately high (2.8) and the greenhouse is only moderately cold—say 35 F degrees colder than the south rooms. The heat loss is thus:

$$(290 \text{ ft.}^2)(35°F)(1/2.8)[\text{Btu}/(\text{ft.}^2 \text{ °F})]$$
$$= \text{about } 3,600 \text{ Btu per hour}$$
$$\text{and}$$
$$14(3,600) = \text{about } 50,000 \text{ Btu}$$
$$\text{per 14-hour night}$$

Direct Gain

About half of the 300,000 Btu incident on the thermosyphoning windows each sunny day in December is transmitted and enters the rooms, thus constituting a direct gain there of about 150,000 Btu. Even on an overcast day the gain through this window system—of the order of 20,000 Btu per day—is significant.

CALCULATIONS CONCERNING OTHER GAINS AND LOSSES

Nonsouth Windows

I assume that these windows, with their R-value of 4.5, roughly break even throughout the winter, as regards solar energy intake and heat loss.

Insulated Walls, North Roof, and Gables

The heavily insulated east, west, and north walls (R-24) lose only about 3,000 Btu per typical hour (75,000 Btu per typical 24-hour-day) in midwinter. The heavily insulated north roof and gables (R-45) lose about the same amount; the area is slightly greater, the ΔT is about twice as great, and the conductance is about half as great.

Fresh-Air Intake

At times when the forced intake of fresh air via the heat exchanger is at the rate of 80 cfm, the outdoor temperature is 20°F, and the air entering the house proper is at about 23°F, the heat load on the house proper (due to this air intake) is about

$$(80\ \text{cfm})(0.08\ \text{lb./ft.}^3)(0.24\ \text{Btu/lb. °F})$$
$$(70°F - 23°F) = 70\ \text{Btu/min.}$$

Thus the heat load for one hour is 4,000 Btu, and for one 24-hour day is 100,000 Btu.

The *average* rate of forced fresh-air intake is about 400 cfm.

(What expense would such a high rate of fresh-air intake entail in a conventional house that had no air-to-air heat exchanger and employed electrical heating at the rate of 10¢/kWh? If the indoor and outdoor temperatures were 70°F and 23°F, the 24-hr.-day heat loss resulting from the 400 cfm intake would be 500,000 Btu, or about 150 kWh. Thus the expense would be 10¢ × 150 = $15 per day, or about $2,500 per winter. It is comforting to know that, in Shrewsbury House, the heat loss is made up by the solar heating system and costs nothing. Of course, the $2,500 saving figure is unrealistically large—because in most houses a fresh-air intake rate of 400 cfm is two to four times as large as necessary.)

CALCULATIONS CONCERNING STORAGE

Upper Storage System

The 18,000 lb. of water in this system, when cooling from 140°F to 80°F, gives out about 1,000,000 Btu.

Lower Storage System

The 100 tons of stones, when cooling ten degrees, gives out about 360,000 Btu.

Other Storage

The house itself—its walls, floors, etc.—stores much heat, as do the foundation walls and the earth beneath the lower storage system. The greenhouse earth also stores much heat. Some storage is contributed by the south foundation wall of the greenhouse, especially as it has some insulation on its outdoor (south) side: two plastic sheets and two airspaces above ground and a Styrofoam skirt below ground.

ACTUAL PERFORMANCE IN WINTER

To make a detailed analysis of the actual performance of the Saunders Shrewsbury House during the winter of 1981–1982 is impossible because of these complicating circumstances:

- Although the house was nominally completed in September 1981, various components were not completed until some months later.

- Some imperfections in construction and adjustment existed, and were not corrected until midwinter. The imperfections involved the vapor barrier in the attic, some of the windows, and the controller.

- Various experimental changes were made from time to time in the mode of operation and in the locations of temperature sensors associated with the multipoint recorders of temperature and relative humidity—2-channel recorder, 28-channel recorder.

- In various periods, the occupant family consisted of just one person, and he was away for about ten hours each weekday. Thus the amount of intrinsic heat was especially small.

- The upper storage system was not completed until the end of November, and the month of December was a remarkably cloudy month. Thus with midwinter arriving, that storage system started off cold. (It soon warmed up, however; the late start did no harm.)

- To make a detailed and meaningful analysis of the performance data would be extremely difficult, especially as there are so many modes of solar-energy intake and heat storage, and there is much interaction among modes.

Analysis of performance during the winter of 1982–1983 is difficult because of additional experimental changes made in operating procedures. Fortunately, there is little need for a detailed analysis because of the obviously excellent general outcomes. Specifically:

- The temperatures in all rooms remained close to 70°F at all times.

- The relative humidity remained within, or close to, the 40% to 50% range.

- The greenhouse temperature never fell as low as 32°F.*

- Fresh air was supplied to the house steadily.

- There were no emergencies, no large excursions of temperature or humidity, no dramatic failures. The system continued to operate well, quietly, and unobtrusively.

- No auxiliary heat was used, except for a brief use of electrical heat to make a bathroom extra warm and to dry paint. (There is no furnace, no fireplace, no wood stove.)

* There was one exception. The first fan motor used was of inappropriate type and failed, allowing the greenhouse temperature to fall below 32°F. A more efficient fan motor was obtained and it performed without incident.

ACTUAL PERFORMANCE IN SUMMER

During the summer of 1982 the house remained cool. Most of the time the rooms were cooler than 75°F, and only on a few occasions did room temperature reach 80°F.

Because the house remained so cool, no formal trials of the available options for improving the cooling were undertaken, thus no formal comparisons of the options were made.

The good performance prevailed despite some handicaps: (1) during most days the house was unoccupied during the daytime and the greenhouse doors to the outdoors were left closed; (2) the intervening, absorbing plastic sheets for the south windows of the rooms were not installed until the end of summer, thus much more solar radiation entered the rooms than had been intended.

It was found desirable to open—at most—only one of the four vents of the main attic. In July, with no vent open, the typical temperature of the attic air was 100° to 130°F. This is high enough to provide considerable solar preheating to the DHW supply, yet low enough that the amount of heat escaping downward into the second-story rooms was trivial, thanks to the helpful stratification and the 3-in. layer of fiberglass. (The reader will remember that the attic solar aperture admits very little solar radiation in summer, and the attic is very well insulated. If the louvers of the Solar Staircase were ever removed in summer, the four vents would be essential to prevent serious overheating of the attic.)

Chapter 15

COST

The cost of the Shrewsbury House, not including the cost of land, garage, architect's fee, solar designer's fee, or painting (the painting was done by the occupant) was about $90,000.

It is said that, on completing the house, the builder announced that he "would do it again for about the same price."

Note that the house, although conceptually complicated and involving lots of strange new components for collecting and saving heat, consists mainly of simple components that are simply assembled:

- water in glass carboys (the carboys are said to cost about $8 if new but only a small fraction of this if obtained secondhand from certain chemical companies)

- stones

- glass sheets of standard types and sizes

- plastic sheets, most of which are of common type

- standard ¼-HP fan

- standard insulating materials—fiberglass, Styrofoam, Thermax

Inspecting the house in detail, one finds practically nothing that qualifies as *high-tech*, or costly. The control device that governs fan speed is special, but neither large, complicated, nor expensive.

Nearly all of the components are fully understandable to a typical contractor, easily procured or easily assembled on-site. There is practically nothing to analyze, adjust, or de-bug. How can one adjust or de-bug air, stones, glass, or plastic?

One could characterize the solar heating system as one that (a) was given much hard and complicated thought in order that (b) the heating system itself would be simple, durable, and inexpensive.

Annual Operating Cost

The annual cost of operating the fan is about $70, assuming electrical power at about 10¢/kWh.

Offsetting this cost is the annual $300 saving from solar preheating of the domestic hot water, relative to use of electrical heating.

Chapter 16

DISCUSSION

The solar designer seems to have succeeded. His goals have been met.

- The house is 100% solar heated.

- Operation in winter is fully automatic.

- There are ample window areas on all four sides of the house.

- There is an integral greenhouse.

- Fresh air pours in steadily 24 hours a day.

- The cost of the house was about the same as that of a conventional house of similar size and comfort.

Furthermore, the Shrewsbury House appears to outperform typical houses of the main competing types.

Ordinary direct-gain passive house: Its limitations—about a dozen of them—are listed in chapter 2. The Shrewsbury House avoids these limitations.

Ordinary indirect-gain passive house: Its limitations, also, are listed in chapter 2. The Shrewsbury House avoids them.

Superinsulated house: It has eight to ten limitations, listed in chapter 2. The Shrewsbury House does not have these limitations.

Double-envelope house: Its six to eight limitations, listed in chapter 2, do not apply to the Shrewsbury House.

Earth-sheltered house: It has about seven limitations. Shrewsbury House has none of them.

IS THE SHREWSBURY HOUSE OVERDESIGNED?

My guess is *yes*. My impression is that the solar designer erred on the side of caution. Perhaps he included more energy-collecting and energy-saving strategies than were needed; or perhaps he designed each component for somewhat higher performance than was needed. One is tempted to say that the house is "110% solar heated"—it seems to have heat to spare!

Employing overdesign was, I suspect, a good idea. First, the overdesign provides assurance of excellent performance—even if some minor shortcomings were to crop up. Second, if each component is overdesigned, the designer can see its full potential and, in designing a subsequent house, he can place more reliance on one component and make certain other components are smaller and less expensive.

I have learned that Saunders has developed the following rule of thumb for houses that are to be 100% solar heated: arrange for the solar energy input in a typical December to be 40% greater than needed in such a month, and you will then find that 100% solar heating will be achieved even in midwinter months that have very unfavorable weather.

Note that overdesign may increase construction cost only slightly. Consider, for example, the construction of the bin of stones: if the contractor installs 100 tons of stones instead of 50 tons, the cost is only a little greater.

IS THE SHREWSBURY HOUSE DESIGN IMMEDIATELY APPLICABLE TO MANY OTHER HOUSES?

In general, no. Houses in different climates require, I understand, slightly different designs. Also houses of different sizes, or houses that will be used by families of different sizes and different lifestyles, will require slightly different designs.

The point is, of course, that the house and its solar heating system embrace so many different components, and the components interact so much, that careful thought must be given to each new house-design project to make sure that the components match both the external parameters and one another. By working out an exact match, the designer insures good performance and minimizes expense.

Saunders has stated that 100% solar heating can be achieved (with a house of the general type exemplified by Shrewsbury House) almost anywhere in the United States, provided the design is adjusted to the latitude and climate pertinent to the chosen site.

DESIGN VARIATIONS

I understand that a number of design variations may be entertained. Questions such as these come to mind:

• Could a successful house of this same general type be built without an integral greenhouse?

• Could the attic collection and storage system be made a lot smaller—especially if the thermosyphoning window system were made a lot larger? Could the attic solar aperture be eliminated?

- Under what circumstances would it be cost-effective to provide thermal shutters for all the external windows?

- Would it pay to design a control system that would take into account temperatures at more locations and distribute heat in a more flexible and versatile way?

- How should the design be modified for application to a much smaller house? A much larger house? A large commercial building?

- How should it be modified for application to a one-story house? A three-story house?

- How should it be modified for application in a colder climate? In a less sunny climate?

- If a developer were to build 100 such houses, what design changes—or component construction changes—might lead to reductions in cost? How would one go about applying "mass production" to such houses and their special components?

The fact is that, even before Shrewsbury House was completed, Saunders was busy trying to work out improved designs. Soon he was hard at work designing Cliff House and All-Solar-Too House. They have exciting new features—explained in the following chapters.

II
CLIFF HOUSE

Chapter 17

CLIFF HOUSE: A GENERAL OVERVIEW

Cliff House, designed and built *after* Shrewsbury House, has some highly desirable features not found in Shrewsbury House.

While approximately equaling Shrewsbury House in being 100% solar heated and having no furnace or wood stove and being almost fully automatic in operation, Cliff House has these advantages:

- It has a very normal appearance—no glass roof.

- It gives the architect an almost free hand in choosing the shape of the house, provided that it has the general form of a rectangular parallelepiped (shoe box), and choosing the layout of the rooms.

- It has independent heating and cooling controls.

- The sunspace is larger and more livable.

- Split-level design is avoided. Entrance to the main story is on-grade.

- One does not have to enter the house via the sunspace.

These features, which may have great appeal not only to prospective owners but also to architects, are discussed in detail in a later section.

A special constraint on the construction of Cliff House is that the actual rate of heat loss must not greatly exceed the nominal (planned) rate. The infiltration rate must be kept very low and the insulation must be installed with care—with no gaps. The margin of safety for achieving 100% solar heating is modest (about 20% for a typical December) and accordingly no gross excess of heat loss can be tolerated. (For Shrewsbury House the margin of safety is larger, about 40%.) Saunders has concluded that, in general, one of the greatest sources of worry to a solar engineer planning for 100% solar heating is uncertainty as to the extent to which the actual rate of heat loss will exceed the nominal (planned) rate. The vagaries of weather

are fairly well understood, but the vagaries of vapor barrier and insulation installation are sometimes unpredictable.

NOTE: This chapter is written as if the
house were complete. This makes the
account shorter and simpler. In fact, as
of May 1983, some details of construction and solar design were not complete. Some of the facts presented concerning design details are merely my
best guesses as to what will become re-
ality. Basic construction of the house
and the basic solar design are complete.
Therefore, in view of the great novelty
and promise of the overall project, it
seemed appropriate to include this account although some of the details are
not final.

GENERAL DESCRIPTION

Cliff House is situated on a 40-ft.-high,
south-facing cliff or ledge in Weston,
Massachusetts, about 12 miles west of
the center of Boston. A flat lawn extends 40 ft. south of the houe, and beyond that the ground falls off steeply. It
is a windy location; there are no tall
trees to the west or south of the house.
It is a 6,000-degree-day (Fahrenheit) location.

This is a two-story, wood-frame, 3-
bedroom, 2½-bathroom house with a
large integral sunspace on the south
and an attached two-car garage on the
east. There is an attic, but no basement;
ledge rock lies a few feet below the first-
story floor.

The living area dimensions are 38
ft. × 28 ft. Thus the floor area of the two-
story living region is $2 \times 38 \times 28 = 2,128$
sq. ft. If one adds the 456 sq. ft. area of
the 38 ft. × 12 ft. sunspace, one arrives
at a total area of 2,584 sq. ft. If one adds
also the 624 sq. ft. of the 26 ft. × 24 ft.
garage, one arrives at an overall floor
area of 3,664 sq. ft.

The house is based on a general design by Edward F. Szabo, an architect
residing in Waltham, Massachusetts.

The general shape of the house, the orientation, the exact location, and the solar heating features were specified by
N. B. Saunders. Because the solar heating features called for did not involve
the living region of the house (except
for the provision of two ducts and two
fans), the architect enjoyed great freedom in laying out the living region.

The main solar features include:

- an extremely large glazed area of the
  vertical south wall of the clerestory
  sunspace that serves as a solar collector and also a comfortable lounge
  area

- an upper storage system in the attic

- a lower storage system extending under the entire living region

- a main airflow system

- a solar-heated domestic hot-water
  system

The builder, Antonio Pulsone, is also
the owner. He and his family will occupy the house.

The cost, not including land or architect's fee or solar designer's fee, would have been about $120,000 if a typical general contractor had been used. Because the owner served as general contractor, did much of the work himself, and showed much ingenuity in minimizing materials and labor costs, the actual cost is probably considerably less than this.

The following drawings show the general layout of the house.

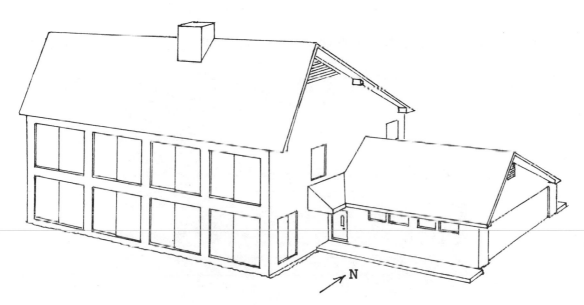

Perspective view of Cliff House, looking northwest.

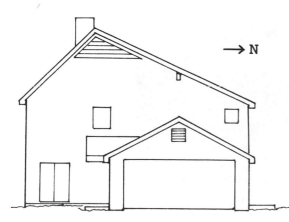

East elevation, looking west.

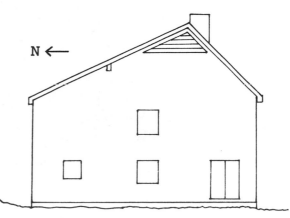

West elevation, looking east.

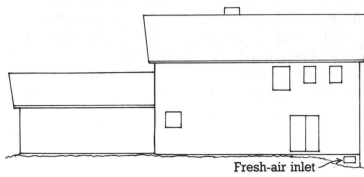

North elevation, looking south.

South face of Cliff House sunspace, showing
the eight double-glazed windows.

East end of Cliff House and attached
two-car garage.

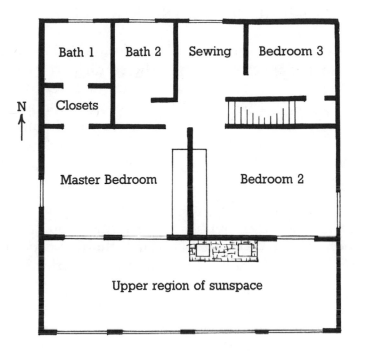

Second-story plan.

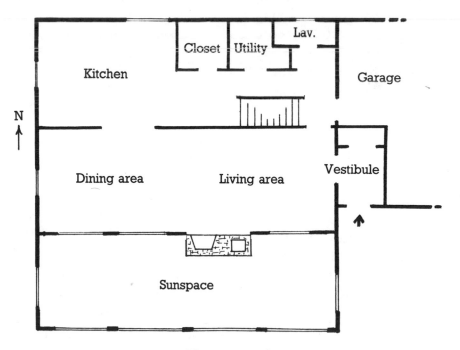

First-story plan.

GENERAL GOALS AND STRATEGIES

Many of the general goals have been listed in chapter 3—goals applicable to all three houses.

Some *goals* specific to Cliff House are:

> To provide a large integral sunspace for sunning, general living, etc. Any use for growing plants is secondary.

> To arrange for the house as a whole to have a very normal appearance—normal-appearing roof (no glazing or panels on the roof).

A major personal goal of the solar designer was to achieve 100% solar heating *without appreciably restricting the architect*. The architect was to be free to choose the number of rooms, the shapes and sizes of the rooms, the materials used in room floors, walls, etc. In other words, the design of the living areas was *not* to be dominated by considerations of solar energy intake, solar energy storage, or energy conservation. (Such considerations were to apply only to the attic, the space beneath the lower floor, and a portion of the sunspace.)

The main *strategies* specific to Cliff House are:

- Use the sunspace itself as the collector of moderately high-temperature heat and yet at the same time keep most of the sunspace region at a temperature below 80°F agreeable to persons sitting or walking about there.

- Arrange for a highly localized, gravity-convective flow of air within the sunspace to carry the collected solar energy (in the form of air at a temperature of 80° to 140°F) upward into the south part of the attic. Also, arrange for a return flow to the sunspace and arrange for this air to be relatively cool (such as 65° to 75°F) to help keep most of the sunspace region cool enough for the comfort of people there.

- Install, in the south part of the attic, an upper storage system that has a large thermal capacity (25,000 Btu/°F) and large surface area (1,800 sq. ft.) and has a high degree of thermal stratification.

- Install, under the first-story floor, a lower storage system that has an even greater thermal capacity (60,000 Btu/°F), a much greater surface area (30,000 sq. ft.) and is thermally stratified. The typical temperature of this system, in winter, is to be 60° to 75°F.

- Provide two automatically controlled, variable-speed fans (and suitable ducts and controls) capable of performing any of the following functions as required for maintaining comfort in the rooms:

> delivery of warm attic air to the rooms,

> delivery of warm attic air to the lower storage system,

> delivery of cool air from the coolest region of the lower storage system to the rooms.

NOTE: Saunders has applied for a patent on airflow control systems having these capabilities.

COMMENTS ON THE TWO STORAGE SYSTEMS

The upper and lower storage systems are very different in function and composition. An understanding of these differences is essential to an understanding of how the system as a whole can provide 100% solar heating and can keep room temperatures close to ideal in winter and summer.

Upper System

This system must be lightweight because (1) it is high up; (2) requires a strong support system; and (3) the incremental cost of the extra support must be kept small (of the order of $500 to $1,000). Accordingly, water is used; it has much greater thermal capacity (Btu's per lb.) than any other low-cost storage material. Because a high degree of thermal stratification exists in this storage system (upper part very hot, lower part relatively cool), much insulation must be used above it but a modest amount of insulation may be used below it.

Because it is fully permissible for this system to undergo large temperature swings, there is no need for the system to have exceptionally large surface area (for exchange of heat with the air passing through it); a total surface area of about 1,800 sq. ft. may be enough.

Lower System

Because this system rests directly on the ground (on ledge rock, moreover), support is positive and free. Thus the use of an enormous weight of storage material—say 100 tons—is permissible. In particular, it is permissible to use stones, even though, pound for pound, they have only one-fifth to one-sixth the thermal capacity of water. The decision to use stones opens the door to a large benefit: by using stones only a few inches in diameter, the designer achieves a total surface of about 30,000 sq. ft.—a truly enormous area. Because the area is so great, the ΔT penalty during heat transfer from the air to the stones (or vice versa) is negligible (less than one Fahrenheit degree). And because this penalty is negligible, keeping the uppermost portion of the bin of stones (and the first-story concrete floor immediately above it) very close to 70°F is feasible irrespective of whether the temperature of the "parent" upper storage system is fairly high (say 130°F) or fairly low (say 85°F).

Because the uppermost portion of the bin and the concrete floor above it are nearly always close to 70°F, they can be relied on to perform two very different—two opposite—functions: (1) *warming* the first-story air whenever that air threatens to become cooler than 70°F, and (2) *cooling* that air whenever it threatens to become hotter than 75°F. Even if, on a single day in winter, the rooms threaten in the morning to be too cold and in the afternoon to become too hot, the thermal mass in question can provide heat in the morning and cooling in the afternoon and thus keep the rooms comfortable at all times. All this is possible because of the large thermal mass and large heat-transfer surface of the bin of stones and the concrete floor.

Clearly, it would be intolerable for the

lower storage system to become much hotter than 75°F. It would quickly overheat the lower rooms (by convection and radiation), and the overly hot air here would rise into the second-story rooms, making them too hot.

In summary, the two stories of living space are sandwiched between an upper and a lower storage system, each of which is designed in a special way to perform its special functions. The combination has instant two-way capability: the upper storage system is ready at all times to immediately deliver heat and the lower storage system is ready at all times to oppose *underheating or overheating*.

Note that practically all other solar-heated houses lack this two-way capability. A typical house has only one storage system, and in winter this system is kept hot and so is incapable of preventing room overheating on a warm day in March, say. In summer it is kept cool and so is of no help at all if, on a cold evening in June, the rooms become too cold. The fact is that, in spring and fall, a few hot days may be followed by a few cold days, or vice versa, and many solar-heating systems are incapable of dealing with such a situation. Therefore, a typical solar house needs an auxiliary heating system to handle sudden cold spells and may need an auxiliary cooling system to help out on hot spells. Opening windows is not effective (for cooling) if the outdoor temperature is 90°F.

The design of Cliff House is such that room temperature remains close to the desired temperature even when several hot days are followed by several cold days; and there is no need for the occupant to operate any controls inasmuch as operation is automatic, as explained on page 110. (The occupant must make certain adjustments each fall and each spring; but no day-to-day adjustments are required.)

As explained in later sections, thermal stratification within each storage system is encouraged, i.e., enhanced by the heat-input flow patterns and also by the heat-output flow patterns. The stratification is essential to the overall versatility and efficiency of the temperature control system.

Chapter 18

SUNSPACE

The most important and most interesting component of the solar heating system of Cliff House is the large integral sunspace, which itself serves as a solar collector.

The sunspace is designed to meet these two seemingly incompatible requirements:

• At times when it receives much solar radiation, it must absorb most of the radiation and transfer most of the resulting heat to air within the sunspace. This heated air then flows up-ward to the sunspace ceiling, passes upward through a slot in the ceiling, and streams into and through the upper storage system, situated in the south half of the attic.

• The lower northern portion of the sunspace must at all times remain cool enough (below 80°F) to be comfortable to the people there.

Later paragraphs explain how these apparently incompatible goals are achieved.

OVERALL DIMENSIONS

The sunspace is as long as the house proper, i.e., 38 ft. It is two stories (18 ft.) high, i.e., of clerestory type, and 12 ft. in north-south dimension.

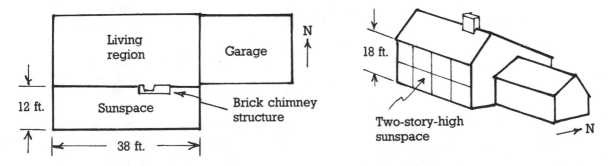

Diagrams showing the dimensions of the integral, south, two-story sunspace.

GLAZING

The total area of glazing of the outer walls of the sunspace is 450 sq. ft. This includes:

	Net glazed area (ft.^{2})
south-facing glazing	400
east-facing glazing	25
west-facing glazing	25
Total	450

The south face of the sunspace consists mainly of eight large vertical windows—four in the lower row and four in the upper row. Each of the windows consists of two large panels of glass that are of sliding-door type; that is, they are framed and mounted on rails just as sliding door panels are. However, to eliminate air leakage at the panel edges,

the builder intends to seal the panels in shut position. Each of the eight windows is 8 ft. wide by 6 ft. 4 in. high and the total area of the set of eight is 400 sq. ft.

Each panel consists of two sheets of iron-free, water-white, $3/16$-in.-thick tempered glass with a $3/8$-in. airspace between. The transmittance of each such panel with respect to solar radiation incident within 30° of the normal is 77%. The R-value of the panel is 1.9.

The east door of the sunspace consists of two double-glazed sliding glass panels. Net area: 25 sq. ft. The transmittance and R-value are the same as for the south windows.

The west door of the sunspace is identical to the east door.

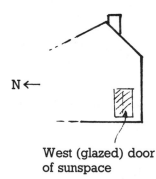

West (glazed) door of sunspace

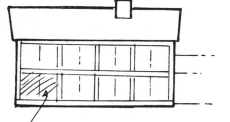

One of the eight south windows of the sunspace

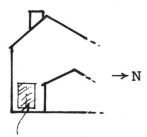

East (glazed) door of sunspace

FLOOR

The sunspace floor consists of a pile rug resting on a 4-in. concrete slab faced with stone tile. As far as solar heating is concerned, the color of the tile is not

important inasmuch as little or no direct solar radiation will strike it. (Such radiation strikes a *special interception system* discussed in a later section.)

NORTH WALL

The north wall of the sunspace includes a massive chimney structure and six large glazed areas serving the lower and upper south rooms, providing them with daylight, view, and a little direct solar heating. Each of the six glazed areas consists of sliding glass doors, each of which is double glazed.

The owner may later install, in the north region of the sunspace, a shallow (2 or 3 ft. wide) balcony to serve some of the upper-story south rooms.

ft.-wide fireplace serving the 38-ft.long living-dining room. The flue for the fireplace is within the west region of the chimney structure. Within the east portion of the chimney structure there is a 2 ft. × 2 ft. cross section vertical duct. There is no definite plan to use this duct, but it may later be put to trial use to help with cooling, as explained in a later section.

Made of ordinary red brick, the chimney structure (not counting the portion within or above the attic) has a mass of about 20,000 lb. and a thermal capacity of about 4,000 Btu/°F.

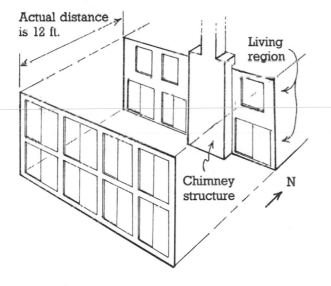

Exploded view showing the relationship of the south facade of the house as a whole to the south facade of the living region.

The chimney structure in the sunspace is 8 ft. wide and 3 ft. thick. At the level of the attic floor the width decreases from 8 ft. to 4 ft. The north face of the chimney structure includes a 3-

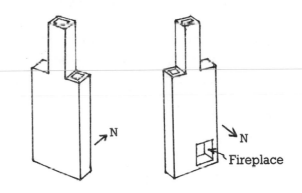

South face.   North face.

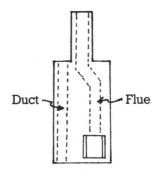

X-ray view, looking south.

INTERCEPTOR SYSTEM

Crucial to the entire collection and storage of solar energy is the interceptor system: a large-area, low-mass system that intercepts most of the solar radiation that enters the sunspace, converts this radiation into heat energy, and promptly transfers the heat to the air. The hot air rises, enters the south region of the attic, and imparts much of its heat to the upper storage system there.

Notice that if any substantial fraction of the solar radiation were to strike the sunspace floor, sunspace north wall, or the brick chimney structure, it would warm them increasingly and, before long, the sunspace as a whole would be too hot for comfort. It is essential that most of the solar radiation be intercepted and that its energy be imparted to a localized upward-flowing stream of air—not to the sunspace floor, walls, etc.

Of course, the interception must not be so complete that the sunspace remains dark or that the people there find their view of the outdoors blocked. The interception system must be designed so as to (a) intercept and absorb about 80% to 90% of the solar radiation entering the sunspace via the south windows, yet (b) allow about 10% to 20% to penetrate deep into the sunspace (and in a widely distributed manner) so as to provide daylighting and view.

The interception system may consist mainly of an array of 400 slender vertical vanes, each 15 ft. high, 4 in. wide, and 0.005 in. thick, situated (in the sunspace) 1 or 2 ft. north of the sunspace south windows. Normally the vanes are parallel to one another and, often, may be oriented parallel to a vertical north-south plane. Each vane is dark greenish gray in color; a chrome green pigment is used because of its special property of absorbing nearly all of the near-infrared portion of the solar spectrum while reflecting a moderately large fraction of the visually important portion (central portion) of the visual-range radiation.

By pulling on a cord, a sunspace occupant can change the orientation of the vanes. While remaining vertical, they can be turned so as to pass more than 95% of the direct rays from the sun, or turned so as to block such rays almost completely. Or the occupant may change the orientation so as to favor some chosen view.

Typically (in winter) the chosen orientation is one that causes 80% to 90% of the solar radiation reaching the array of vanes to be absorbed by them, while about 10% to 20% of the radiation passes through. Thanks to the selective properties of the pigment used on the vanes, the visual transmittance of the array considerably exceeds 10% to 20%; it may be 20% to 35%, and accordingly the array does not appear dark or gloomy.

During a sunny noontime in January the vanes receive and absorb much solar radiation, become very hot, and so heat the adjacent air. Result: a strong upward flow of very hot air in the immediate vicinity of the vanes. The up-

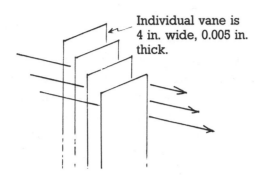

Perspective view of a few vanes, showing rays passing straight through.

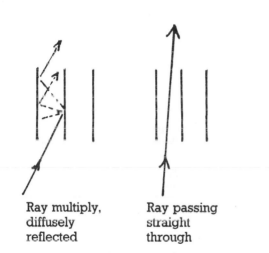

Ray multiply, diffusely reflected

Ray passing straight through

Plan view of a few of the vanes.

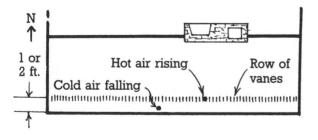

Plan view of the sunspace, showing the location of the row of vertical vanes.

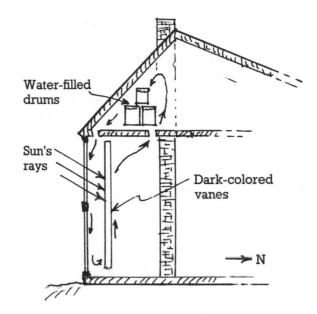

Vertical cross section of the sunspace and upper storage system, showing the paths of airflow on a sunny day in winter. Schematic only.

ward-streaming hot air, on approaching the sunspace ceiling, turns and flows northward a few feet and enters the south part of the attic (via a 34-ft.-long, 6-in.-wide slot) near the northern limit thereof. (See the diagram.) The airflow is, of course, entirely passive.

The array of vanes is sufficiently far from the sunspace south windows (1 or 2 ft. away) that the upward flow of air is well clear of the *downward* flow of cool air traveling within 2 in. of those windows. This downward flowing air (*return* air) travels from the south part of the attic (the upper storage system) via a slot situated close to the south edge of the attic, i.e., almost directly above the set of sunspace south windows.

Notice that, in a sense, the looplike airflow in the sunspace is a *reverse* flow:

air close to the south windows descends, air farther from the south windows ascends. This is what one would expect to happen at night; but for it to happen on a sunny day is unusual. Why does it occur? Because the very hot interceptor array is far to the north of the windows and is much hotter than the window glass.

Notice also that the flow is entirely passive; it is a thermosyphon flow, i.e., a gravity-convective flow.

Notice, finally, that this flow is independent of flows involving the living area of the house or involving the bin of stones. As long as all the doors and windows between the rooms and sunspace remain closed, no air flows from the sunspace to the rooms or vice versa.

Chapter 19

THERMAL–STORAGE SYSTEMS

UPPER STORAGE SYSTEM

The purpose of the upper storage system is to store a large amount of heat at moderately high temperature, such as 80° to 130°F.

Location and Components

The system is situated in the south part of the attic and is enclosed in insulation. The floor of this part of the attic is insulated with fiberglass to R-19, and the storage system is covered with a 6-in.-thick, R-19 cocoon of fiberglass. In addition, the attic roof and end walls are insulated with fiberglass to R-30.

The system includes 10 tons (20,000 lb.) of ordinary water. There is no antifreeze, nothing to control pH, corrosion, or growth of algae. The enclosing structure adds slightly to the thermal mass.

The containers are secondhand 55-gal. plastic drums—fifty in all. The total nominal capacity is 2,750 gal. and the total effective surface area, including that of the enclosure, is 1,800 ft.^{2}. The containers are arranged in two tiers: lower and upper. The lower tier in-

cludes two side-by-side rows and the upper tier includes one row. The spaces between the drums measure about 2 in.—ample to allow free airflow.

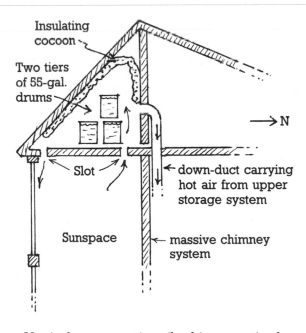

Vertical cross section (looking west) of the south part of the attic and the upper storage system.

Operation

The hot air from the sunspace enters the upper storage system along such a path that this air makes contact first with the *upper* row of water-filled drums—the hottest ones. After giving up some heat and cooling somewhat, the air descends by gravity convection and contacts the lower rows of drums, delivering heat to them. In other words, the flow path is such as to maintain and even enhance the thermal stratification in this storage system.

Actually, there is an additional way in which the stratification is enhanced: the air contacts the upper portion of each drum before descending and making contact with the lower portion. Thus even the within-drum stratification is enhanced.

The obvious consequences are: (1) the uppermost region of the storage system may be very hot, such as 135°F; (2) the lowest region may be cool, such as 60°F; and (3) the air that (after surrendering its heat) descends into the sunspace is cool—cool enough to counteract any tendency of the air in the lower region

of the sunspace (region where people are) to become too hot for comfort.

(As I point out on a later page, the thermal stratification is enhanced not only by the flow path of hot air from the sunspace but also by the flow path of cool air traveling upward via the stair-wells. There are two enhancement processes at work!)

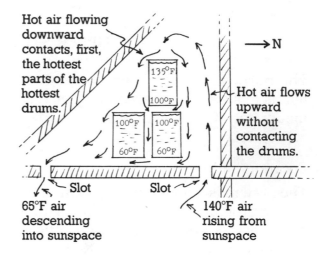

Highly simplified diagram showing how the flow path of the hot air from the sunspace enhances the thermal stratification of the upper storage system.

LOWER STORAGE SYSTEM

Location and Components

The lower storage system consists of (1) a large quantity of stones situated beneath the living-area first-story floor (a 4-in.-thick concrete floor) and (2) this floor itself. Ledge rock beneath the stones contributes only very slightly. Plan-view dimensions of the storage system are 37 ft. × 27 ft.

Purpose

The main purpose of the lower storage system is to *regulate* temperature, that is, to keep the temperature of the first-story air close to 70°F—to prevent the temperature from rising much above this on sunny days (when much solar radiation passes clean through the sunspace and enters the living area rooms) or falling much below this on cold nights.

In the short term, the regulation is due mainly to the large thermal capacity of the lower storage system and the concrete floor and also to the large area of the floor. The floor exchanges energy with the rooms by convection and radiation.

In the longer term, the regulation depends in large part on the large heat-transfer area of the quantity of stones. If, for example, the stones threaten to become too cold, they can be heated up fairly quickly by an accelerated flow of warm air from the upper storage system. They can be heated fairly quickly even if the upper storage system is only moderately hot—thanks to the huge surface area of the stones and the consequent small ΔT penalty.

Main Features

The 100-ton quantity of stones has a thermal capacity of about 35,000 Btu/°F. This is augmented by the effective thermal capacity of the enclosing foundation walls, underlying ledge rock, etc., with the consequence that the overall effective thermal capacity is about 60,000 Btu/°F.

The effective surface area is about 50,000 sq. ft.

No vapor barrier is used under or above the stones. No moisture problem is expected inasmuch as the house rests on ledge rock, is on a cliff, and the foundation walls are flanked by drainpipes.

Note that no special housing is provided for the stones. The foundation walls themselves, together with the special wall beneath the north edge of the sunspace, serve as housing.

Chapter 20

MAIN AIRFLOW SYSTEM

Two forced-airflow circuits serve to distribute hot air from the upper storage system. The two streams start off together: they travel together vertically downward in a 10-ft.-long duct originating at a location immediately to the north of the mid-region of the upper storage system. The flow is forced by the *upper fan* discussed in a later section.

The flow then divides into two delivery paths:

1. first-story delivery path, resulting in delivery of hot air to the first-story rooms

2. subfloor delivery path, resulting in delivery of hot air to the lower-story subfloor space, i.e., to the bin of stones

FUNCTIONS OF THE TWO FORCED-AIRFLOW CIRCUITS

The function of the first-story delivery is obvious enough: the flow of hot air from the upper storage system to the first-story rooms warms these rooms, and the subsequent flow of warm air up the stairwell to the upper story warms the upper-story rooms.

The function of the subfloor delivery is not so obvious. There are, in fact, two functions: (1) to warm the bin of stones, or rather, to warm a large fraction of it, and (2) to *cool* the rooms if they are too warm. How can one flow of hot air perform these two functions? In particular, how can it *cool* a room? It can do all of these things by virtue of the fact that the bin of stones is not thermally homogenous: the part the hot air pervades first (upper central part) is warm, but the part that it encounters last (lower peripheral part) is cool. (The air that enters the bin of stones and then travels laterally and slightly downward tends to become cooler as it travels along.) Thus the process of driving hot air into the warm part of the bin has the consequence of driving cool air out of the cool portion of the bin—and into the first-story rooms. After cooling these rooms, the cool air passes up the lower stair-well and cools the upper-story rooms. In summary, it cools both stories. It returns to the attic via the upper stairwell.

THE FLOW PATHS OF DOWNWARD-MOVING AIR

Air leaves the upper storage system at the north side thereof and at a level about two-thirds of the way from the bottom to top of the system. Thus the air is taken from the hotter (i.e., upper) half of the region, but not from the very hottest (uppermost) part. The uppermost part is reserved for extraction of heat by the pipes that preheat the domestic hot water supply.

The air flows vertically downward via a 10 ft. long duct that is 2 ft. × 2 ft. in cross section. Then it turns and starts to flow northward in two parallel, horizontal, between-joists ducts each of which is 1 ft. × 2 ft. in cross section. It then has two choices of path:

1. It can escape downward into the first-story rooms (living-dining room, etc.)

2. It can flow northward to the north wall of the house and then flow downward into the entrance plenum of the lower storage system. (The flowpath within that system is discussed in a later section. Eventually the air emerges into the kitchen.)

The return flows are discussed in a later section.

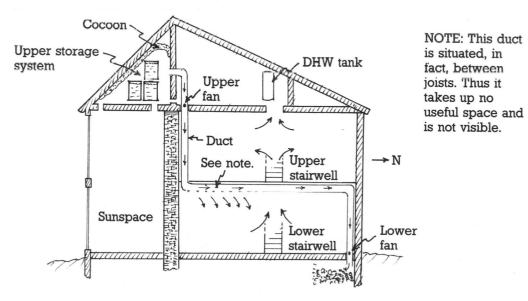

Vertical cross section, looking west, showing the paths of the main airflow.

Where the warm air from the upper storage system enters the first-story rooms (actually the living-dining room), arrangement has been made for the speed of the air entering the room to be very low. If air moving as fast as 5 ft./sec. were to strike people there, they would find the air movement very noticeable and unpleasant. But if it is moving at only ½ ft./sec., they are unaware of it and experience no discomfort. Accordingly, the designer has provided (within the first-story ceiling) two parallel ducts, 3 ft. apart on centers, and each with a screened opening 14 in. wide and 10 ft. long on its underside. Because the total opening is so large, the speed of the air emerging from the opening is only about 0.1 to 1.5 ft./sec., depending on the speeds of the fans. At locations a few feet or more below the ceiling, the speed is much lower: so low that people there are not aware of any air motion.

FANS AND SENSORS

Each fan is rated at ¼ HP and has variable speed.

The *upper fan* is at attic-floor level and drives air downward. It is controlled by a sensor and an electrical circuit in such manner that:

- It stops entirely if the temperature of the lower rooms is above a specified lower point, such as 69°F, as judged by a sensor situated in the living-dining room, close to the lower stairwell.

- It speeds up as the temperature there falls below 69°F and runs at full speed (producing a flow rate of about 1,800 cfm) when that temperature is lower than 63°F.

The *lower fan* is at first-story-floor level and drives air downward into the lower storage system. It is controlled by a sensor and an electrical circuit in such manner that:

- It stops entirely if the temperature of the lower rooms is below a specified upper point, such as 72°F, as judged by a second sensor situated close to the first sensor.

- It speeds up as room temperature rises above 72°F and runs at full speed (producing a flow rate of about 1,800 cfm) when the temperature exceeds 80°F.

NOTE: It may happen that the occupants will prefer a somewhat higher room temperature, inasmuch as the heat is free. Thus they might set the thermostats, not at 69°F and 72°F, but at 75°F and 78°F.

EXCEPTION: Both fans operate when and if the temperature at the top of the upper storage system exceeds a chosen upper limit, such as 145°F. It is expected that this situation will arise seldom, if ever. If it does arise and the rooms then become too hot, the occupants may—to improve comfort—open windows or doors.

FLOW PATH WITHIN BIN OF STONES

When fan-forced warm attic air travels downward and enters the bin of stones, it enters near the center of the north wall of the house via a 4-sq.-ft. opening in the floor of the small closet adjacent to the kitchen. The lower fan is located at this opening, near floor level.

The air first enters an informal inlet plenum, actually a long shallow tongue-shaped hollow in the bin of stones. From here it spreads out in many directions within the bin. While traveling outward from the hollow, it travels slightly downward, losing heat as it goes. Thus the remote, low regions within the bin may remain as cool as 60° or 70°F.

Eventually the air in the bin of stones makes its way to the lower part of the west foundation wall and enters a 27-ft.-long north-south duct. Near the centerpoint of the duct is a branch (an up-duct) that extends upward a few feet and delivers air to the kitchen via a grille beneath a kitchen counter. The duct is three-sided, the sides being (a) the west foundation wall, (b) the surface of the ledge rock, and (c) a row of slanted concrete plates 2 in. thick by 1½ ft. × 2 ft. There are gaps, or "cracks," be-tween plates, and accordingly the duct is "leaky" and serves as a mainfold; air can leak into it (or out of it) along almost its entire length.

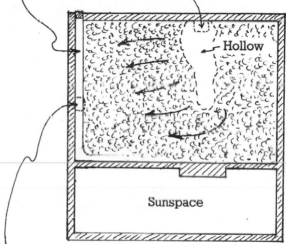

Duct that collects air that has traveled at least 15 or 20 ft. westward and downward within the bin of stones

Here, air flows downward, via an opening in the closet floor, into a hollow in the bin of stones.

Hollow

Sunspace

Here, air from the lowest and coldest part of the bin of stones flows upward into the kitchen.

Horizontal cross section through the bin of stones showing typical airflow paths within the bin.

RETURN FLOW

The warm attic air that is discharged directly into the first-story rooms returns to the attic via the stairwells. First it travels up the stairwell leading to the upper story where it spreads laterally and contributes to keeping the temperature comfortable. Then it travels up the stairwell leading to the attic. It enters the south enclosure (the upper storage system proper) via a slot at the base thereof; accordingly, this air, which is relatively cool, encounters first the lowest (coolest) part of the array of water-filled drums, and extracts some heat from this part—thus helping preserve the thermal stratification.

The air that emerges from the bin of stones into the kitchen follows this same general path; it diffuses through the rooms and travels upward via the stairwells and reenters the upper storage system.

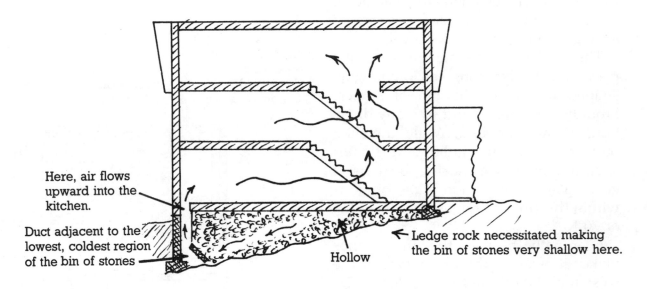

Here, air flows upward into the kitchen.

Duct adjacent to the lowest, coldest region of the bin of stones

Hollow

Ledge rock necessitated making the bin of stones very shallow here.

Vertical cross section, looking north. Highly schematic.
Air returns to the attic via the stairwells.

Note concerning an alternative return path A possible alternative return path for below-first-story air may be used alone or with the path described above. The alternative path would employ (1) a horizontal duct that runs eastward beneath the first-story floor from the above-mentioned west-foundation-wall duct to the base of the massive chimney structure, and (2) the vertical duct incorporated in the east portion of that chimney structure. For further details, see chapter 2 dealing with cooling the house in summer.

Chapter 21

OTHER COMPONENTS

The house has many other interesting components, but they must be described here only briefly.

Vestibule The main entry to the house is via a vestibule that is in the southwest corner of the garage and adjoins the east end of the living dining room.

Wall insulation Typical walls of the house are insulated to about R-30 with 3½ in. of fiberglass and 2 in. of isocyanurate foam. The walls include a single row of 2 × 4s that are 16 in. apart on centers. The foundation walls are insulated externally with 2 in. of Styrofoam.

East, west, and north windows These have a combined area of 108 sq. ft., or about 5% of the floor area of the living portion of the house. All of these windows have multiple glazing (like that of the corresponding windows of Shrewsbury House) of special type that provides an insulation of R-5.

Vapor barrier All of the external walls, and also the attic roof and gables, are covered with a 0.006 in. polyethylene vapor barrier. In a typical external wall, the vapor barrier is close to the warm side of the wall, being covered there only by gypsum board.

Overall tightness of the house Tests made with blowers that pressurize the house indicate that it is reasonably airtight. Under typical conditions of outdoor temperature and wind, the rate of air change is estimated at 0.25 to 0.5 air changes per hour.

Will an air-to-air heat exchanger be needed? The answer will depend on the outcome of infiltration-rate tests planned for the spring of 1983. If an exchanger is needed, it can be installed easily in the attic.

Quantity of stones beneath the sunspace floor About 20 tons of 2-to-4-in. diameter stones are situated immediately beneath the sunspace floor. They will contribute slightly to regulating the temperature of the sunspace floor. Although there is an opening (2 ft. × 2 ft.) between this quantity of stones and the much larger quantity in the lower storage system, the 2 ft. × 2 ft. "return port" to the sunspace has been closed; no complete circulatory path is available and accordingly little heat will flow from the lower storage system to the stones beneath the sunspace floor. It is believed that no circulation of air here is needed. (If it is needed, the return port can be opened. Provision has been made for installing a small fan there. If the lower region of the sunspace becomes too hot, the fan could help by delivering air that, on emerging from the sub-floor stones, is at, or slightly below, 70°F.)

DHW system   The house domestic hot-water supply is solar-preheated by the hot air in the upper storage system. The 80-gal. DHW tank itself is not in upper storage system space—the south attic space. It is in the separately insulated *central* attic room which, typically, is at about 70°F. The tank is well insulated. The solar preheating occurs in the supply line for that tank; this line, situated within the *south* attic space, includes an initial lower segment situated in air that is only moderately hot, and a final upper segment situated in the hottest air. This latter segment includes a small pre-heat tank (about 40 gal.)

Electric heater   At the owner's request, as an added bit of insurance, a 5 kW electric heating element was installed in the attic, at the upper end of the duct that carries hot air downward toward the living-dining room. If for some reason the solar heating system were to fail, this heater could be used to keep the house warm. The expectation is that this heater will not be used.

Vents   At each end of the attic is a vent with an effective clear area of 20 sq. ft. In winter the vents are closed with R-40 covers. In summer the east vent will be opened to permit escape of hot air from the sunspace. (See chapter 23 on summertime cooling.)

Port for intake of outdoor air   Near the west end of the north foundation wall is a screened, 2 ft. × 2 ft. port that is kept closed in winter but is left open in summer to admit cool outdoor air. A small fan may be installed here to insure fast inflow of cold air at night. (See chapter 23 on summertime cooling.)

Computer calculations   In the course of designing the thermal system of Cliff House, and in the course of adjusting and balancing the main parameters, Saunders has made many computer calculations. These give reassurance that the various components will perform about as expected and that, together, they will keep the rooms at about 70°F throughout the winter—even in long, cold, cloudy spells—without the need for auxiliary heat. I do not discuss the computer calculations here, partly because they have not been written up in a formal and understandable manner and partly because many of them were based on various assumptions as to design and construction. Even at this writing (May 1983) some of the design details are still subject to change.

From inspection of some of the calculation procedures, I have learned that they are highly sophisticated. It would be a great mistake for anyone to assume that, because Saunders is very inventive and a great experimenter, his designs are based mainly on intuition, hope, or optimism. Each final design has been eveluted in considerable detail and depth, and embodies much solid engineering.

Chapter 22

WINTERTIME PERFORMANCE

Because, at the time of this writing (May 1983), the construction of the house is not quite complete, and the house has not yet been occupied, and there has been no routine operation of the solar heating system, there is little verified information that can be presented on performance.

The goal of 100% solar heating (with help from intrinsic heat) is expected to be achieved. The overall thermal design was aimed at having, in the most difficult month of the year (December), 20% excess of solar energy intake. Some of this excess will be used if the insulation and airtightness do not conform fully to specifications. Another part of the excess will be used up if some midwinter month happens to have, in some year, a climate much more severe than expected. Specifically, it is expected that, in a typical winter, room temperature will seldom be as low as 67°F and perhaps never will be as low as 62°F.

It is expected that, on very cold nights in winter, the sunspace will cool down almost to 32°F. Heat will be imparted to the sunspace, on such nights, by (1) the thermal mass of the sunspace floor and the massive chimney structure, (2) the south faces of the south living rooms, and (3) the warm ceiling of the sunspace—kept warm by the upper storage system. Nevertheless, the sunspace will lose much heat, via its 450 sq. ft. of double-glazed windows on the south, east, and west.

Relative humidity in the living region is expected to remain, in winter, in the range from 20% to 40%. One factor that tends to keep the value low is the fact that the house is situated on a ledge near the top of a cliff; thus the region below the first-story floor is expected to be relatively dry throughout the winter. If the airtightness of the house turns out to be less than expected, the threat of high relative humidity is practially eliminated.

Other performance characteristics worthy of note are:

• The north living rooms are not slighted: they too remain close to 70°F even in long, cold, cloudy periods.

- There are no noticeable air currents in the living region—even when the fans are operating at maximum power.

- There are adequate window areas on all four sides of the house. Daylighting and view are "all around."

- There are no thermal shades to operate each evening and morning. Thanks to the special designs of the east, west, and north windows (R-value approximately 5), persons sitting close to those windows feel fully comfortable.

- Operation is completely automatic. Even if the occupants are away for a week, the sensors and fans continue to do their jobs, adjusting the air flow rates as required to keep the rooms at about 70°F.

- All of the living region has a fully normal appearance. Nowhere in that region is there a Morse (Trombe) wall, or a wall of water-filled containers, or other special solar paraphernalia.

- The domestic hot-water system will be preheated to a considerable extent by stored solar energy. To what extent? Perhaps 80 to 90%.

- The cost of the house (about $120,000) is about the same as that of a conventional house of comparable size. The saving from having no furnace, no oil tank, no furnace room, no radiators, etc., approximately matches the added cost of special insulation, thermal storage, and fans.

- The annual operating cost will be merely the cost of running the fans, estimated at about $100 per year.

Chapter 23

KEEPING COOL IN SUMMER

The problem of keeping the living region of Cliff House cool in summer is made relatively easy by the facts that (1) almost no solar energy enters the living region from the south because of the protection provided by the sunspace, and (2) the house is very well insulated (walls are well insulated, and east, west, and north windows are of special R-5 type).

The lower region of the bin of stones remains at about 70°F or cooler, and the forced flow of air from this region to the rooms keeps them cooler than 78°F at nearly all times.

If the bin of stones threatens to become too hot, the occupant can open a port at the north end of the north-south subfloor duct and allow cool night air to enter. A special outdoor-air intake fan, situated at this port, can be used to increase the intake of air, a small fraction of which enters the bin of stones directly.

Most of the fan-forced cool air is delivered to the kitchen and to the attic. To reach the attic, the air travels along a west-east subfloor duct and thence up

the duct within the massive chimney structure (a duct that is parallel to the fireplace flue and 3 ft. east of it). The cool air is discharged near the attic floor and, being cool, promptly descends, via the stairwells, to the upper story and lower story, thus cooling both stories.

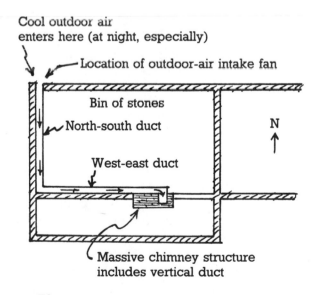

Plan view of the subfloor region of Cliff House, showing the locations of the ducts that carry cool air (on summer nights, for example).

Of course, if the upper storage system threatens to become too hot, the occupants may open one or both of the 20-sq.-ft. vents in the gables. If both vents are open, the prevailing west wind can reduce the temperature rapidly. Because the occupants wish to continue the solar-preheating of the domestic hot water supply, they wish to keep the upper storage system at about 130°F throughout the summer. They may decide to open only one vent, probably the east vent—because (with the prevailing wind coming from the west) the pressure here tends to be slightly negative, facilitating drawing hot air from the sunspace.

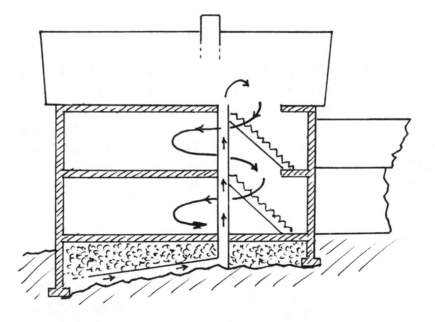

Vertical cross section (highly schematic) looking north, showing locations of some of the main paths of flow of cool air from outdoors on a summer night. One portion of the cool air that enters at the northwest corner of the subfloor region travels 15 ft. south in the north-south duct, then travels upward and emerges into the kitchen. Another portion travels farther south in that duct, then travels 24 ft. east in the west-east duct (shown in diagram), then travels up the duct within the massive chimney structure and emerges into the attic central room. Some of this air then descends via the stairwells, cooling the rooms of both stories en route. Another portion, instead of descending, passes to the outdoors via a gable vent. Note: if the occupants open the west door to the sunspace, cool air will enter here also.

III
ALL-SOLAR-TOO HOUSE

Chapter 24

ALL-SOLAR-TOO HOUSE

All-Solar-Too House, which may be regarded as being, to a moderate extent, a slightly smaller, one-story version of Shrewsbury House, was designed by N. B. Saunders for submission to a 1982 passive-solar-design competition arranged by Garden Way Publishing Co. of Charlotte, Vermont.

The goal was to design an attractive but small (1,000 sq. ft.), one-story house, with a small integral greenhouse, that would be 100% heated by solar energy and intrinsic heat, would be essentially automatic in operation, and would cost about the same as a conventional house of similar size.

No house of this specific type has been built and none is now under construction. Indeed, the results of the competition have not yet been publicized.

The design is, in a sense, a general (open-ended) one. For example, the length of the house can be increased in increments of 4 ft.; the number of roof bays that employ the Solar Staircase℠ can be changed to accommodate different climates; wide variations in room placement and layout are permitted.

What are important, of course, are the principles used, the principles of energy conservation, solar-energy intake, and energy storage.

In the following sections I describe the main goals and design principles. Many of the sections are brief—either because the details are similar to those of Shrewsbury House or because decisions on design details have not yet been made.

GOALS

Many of the design goals are similar to those of Shrewsbury House. A few are similar to those of Cliff House. The main goals include:

- 100% heating by solar energy and intrinsic heat. No furnace, no wood stove.

- A large enough surplus of solar energy intake to accommodate imperfections in installing insulation and in sealing the structure, unusually severe winters, a steady inflow of fresh air, a thermostat setting somewhat higher than that typical of most solar houses.

- Small integral greenhouse.

- Steady inflow of fresh outdoor air.

- Control of humidity.

- Ample window areas even on the east, west, and north sides of the house.

- Control of glare.

- Avoidance of overheating on sunny winter days—as well as in summer.

- Automatic operation such that the occupants have no day-to-day responsibilities and such that even if the occu-

pants are away for a week the rooms will remain near 70°F. Manual readjustment of controls is needed at the start and finish of summer.

- No cold spots near windows; all windows are of special high-R type; no thermal shades or shutters are needed.

- Domestic hot water is almost entirely heated by solar energy.

- In summer, room temperature remains below 80°F. There is no air conditioner.

- The house as a whole is easy to build. It consists mainly of simple components made of durable materials (water, stones, glass, plastic, etc.), and it requires very little maintenance.

- The construction cost is about the same as that of a conventional house of similar size and comfort.

STRATEGIES AND COMPONENTS

The main strategies and components used, many of which are similar to those used in Shrewsbury House or Cliff House, include the following:

- Much use of insulation in the walls, roof, foundation walls, etc., and use of earth berms on the east, west, and north.

- Windows are of special, high-R (R-5) type that can be fully opened and are extremely airtight when closed and locked.

- Carefully sealed vapor barriers are used.

- The small, south, integral greenhouse serves also as an air-lock entrance.

- An 8-ft.-wide region of the south roof is of the Solar Staircase type, admitting much solar radiation in winter, reflecting most such radiation back to the sky in summer, and providing high R-value (R-6).

- Much of the remaining area of the south roof consists of air-type, thermosyphoning solar-energy collectors, which, on sunny days, deliver hot air (at about 130°F, typically) to the upper region of the attic.

- The six exterior vertical south windows of the living region are of special, high-R (R-6) type. Besides providing daylight and view, they perform as (a) air-type solar-energy collectors supplying much hot air to the upper storage system (discussed in a following paragraph), and (b) heat-recovery devices for capturing heat that would otherwise escape via the windows to the outdoors. Because they have low visual transmittance (about 25%), they reduce glare in the south rooms. Because their transmittance with respect to solar radiation (visual range and near-infrared) is appreciable (about 20%), they permit some direct-gain heating of the south rooms.

- An upper storage system in the attic consisting of 13 tons (26,000 lb.) of water in glass carboys and plastic drums. The upper portion of the storage system is, typically, at about 130°F, ready at all times to supply heat. The high degree of thermal stratification in the storage system is helpful.

- A lower storage system, beneath the floor, in the space defined by the foundation walls, consisting of 100 tons of 1-to-3-in. diameter stones. The upper region of the stones, in contact with the 4-in. concrete-slab floor, is at about 70°F and thus is ready at all times to oppose room overheating. The thermal stratification in the storage system is helpful.

- An automatic control system, much like that used in Cliff House, that employs two thermostats and two fans. They operate as follows:

Thermostats One thermostat, perhaps set at 70°F, controls delivery of hot air from the upper storage system. The other, perhaps set at 78°F, controls delivery of hot air to the upper part of the bin of stones and the consequent flow of cool air from the lower part of the bin of stones.

Fans One fan forces the delivery of hot air from the upper storage system and the other forces the delivery of such air to the lower storage system. Each fan, nominally rated at ¼HP, can be *on* or *off*, and when it is *on* the rotational speed is automatically varied so as to keep room temperature near 70°F and perform other functions such as keeping the upper part of the bin of stones at optimum temperature (about 70°F or slightly below) and preventing any excessive temperature rise in the upper storage system. Note that, as in Cliff House, room heating and cooling are controlled positively and independently, and no attention by the house occupants is required; also, warm attic air can be delivered directly to the rooms and/or directly to the bin of stones. At typical times, the fans are operated at about 25 watts each. The annual cost of electricity to run the fans is about $50.

• A within-bin-of-stones airflow-path such that hot attic air enters the bin at an upper north-central location, then flows outward and slightly downward in many directions (becoming gradually cooler), then finds its way into ducts situated along the bases of the east, west, and south foundation walls. This air emerges upward from the south duct and flows either (a) into the greenhouse, to help keep it warm at night, and thence to the outdoors via an opening in the lower part of the greenhouse outer wall, or (b) into the lower end of the vertical south-window structures and then upward into the south-roof air-type collectors.

• A steady flow of fresh outdoor air into the vertical south window structures and thence upward into the south-roof air-type collectors. The upward flow occurs in the outermost of the three airspaces defined by the window's four transparent sheets, and some heat is picked up from the sheet that is immediately adjacent to the north. (See the diagram of the window cross section.) Altogether there are three upward airflows within the window structure, and they intercept (recover) most of the heat that would otherwise escape via the window to the outdoors.

• Each south-roof air-type collector is double glazed, the upper sheet consisting of glass and the lower sheet of Teflon. The black absorber sheet, of aluminum, is spaced 3 in. from the Teflon sheet. On sunny days, hot air

thermosyphoning upward and northward within the collector is discharged into the uppermost part of the attic. The cooler air that enters the lower south end of the collector comes either from the vertical south window structure or (via a plastic-film-type damper) from near the floor of the attic. At night little heat is lost via the collector because (a) much insulation is provided beneath the aluminum absorber sheet and (b) the damper remains shut.

• The domestic hot-water tank is mounted in the upper (hottest) part of the attic, and generous lengths of supply lines are situated here. Thus stored solar energy flows steadily into the DHW system, providing about 80% of the heat needed; the actual figure might be as low as 60% or as high as 100%, depending on the climate, the amount of hot water used, etc.

• If the room-air humidity tends to become too low, it can be increased by supplying a little water to the bin of stones. The water will rest on the vapor barrier between the stones and the ground, and the steady, forced, circulation of air through the bin will evaporate some of the water and carry humid air to the rooms.

• Inflow of fresh outdoor air produces one complete change every two hours—possibly every hour.

• In summer, cold night air can be drawn into the house by the fans via an underground tube at the north of

All-Solar-Too House, perspective view. The south roof and south vertical wall are glazed for collection of solar energy. The two central bays of the south roof are backed by the Solar Staircase™. The attached greenhouse serves as an air-lock entrance. There is no furnace, woodstove, or chimney.

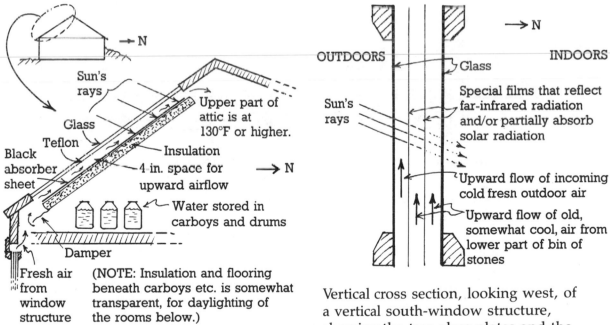

Vertical cross section, looking west, of upper south region of attic, showing the locations of the south-roof air-type collector, damper, and carboys containing water. Schematic; not to scale.

Vertical cross section, looking west, of a vertical south-window structure, showing the two glass plates and the intervening sheets of special plastic, and showing the airflows that intercept (salvage) much of the heat that would otherwise escape via the window to the outdoors. Schematic; not to scale.

the house. Such air can cool the rooms directly and can also cool the bin of stones so that, during a hot day, the rooms can be cooled by a forced flow of air from the bin. Of course, an alternative procedure is to open the outside door and/or the east, west, and north windows. Any of these procedures increases the rate of air change. The bin of stones, espe-

cially the lower part thereof, being cooler than typical indoor air, tends to condense moisture from such air, thus preventing humidity from becoming uncomfortably high.

Many of the main design features are portrayed in the illustrations on pages 125 and 126.

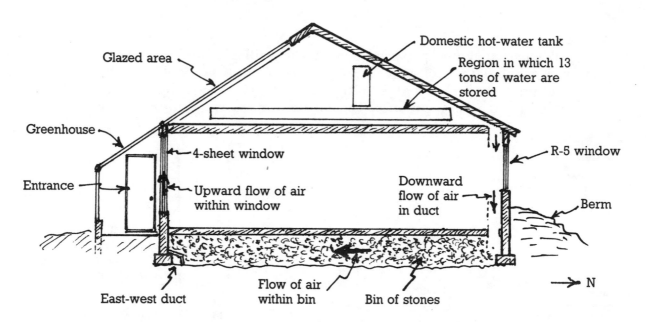

Cross section, looking west. At the extreme right, hot air from the attic flows downward into the rooms and/or into the bin of stones. The upward return flow is within the 4-sheet vertical south window structures. Simplified; not to scale. (Not shown: insulation, fans, damper, and many other components.)

PERFORMANCE

Estimates made by Saunders with the aid of many computer calculations and comparisons with other houses designed by him indicate that there is a

firm expectation that All-Solar-Too House would indeed be 100% heated by solar energy assisted by intrinsic heat. Even in the most difficult month there is a nominal 30% to 40% excess of such energy. Temperature should hold constant near 70°F in the north rooms as well as in the south rooms.

In summer, room temperature would usually be between 70° and 75°F, and in hot spells it would rise to almost 80°F. No air conditioner would be needed.

The annual operating cost is merely the cost of operating the two fans: $50.

The construction cost would be about $50,000, or roughly the same as that of a conventional house of similar size.

The domestic hot water would be about 80% solar heated, representing an annual saving of about $200 relative to use of electricity.

IV
COMPARISON

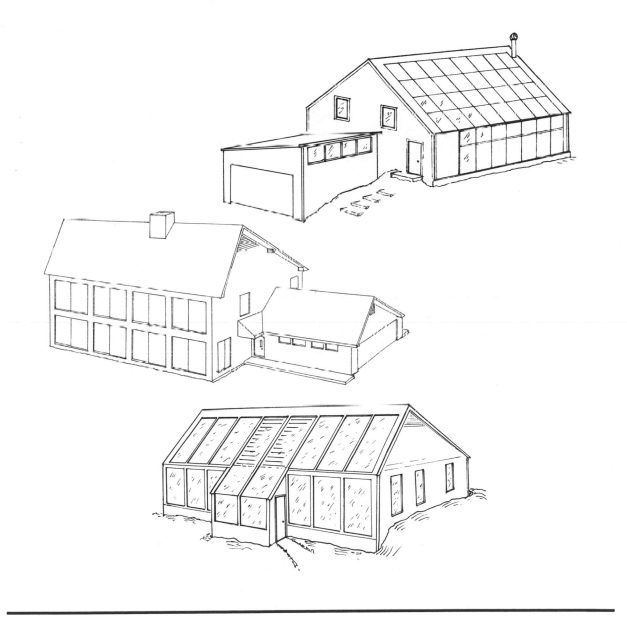

Chapter 25

COMPARISONS OF THE THREE HOUSES

DIFFERENCES

In comparing the three houses, one sees the following differences.

Differences in Emphasis or Priority

In designing Shrewsbury House, the designer focused first on the solar heating system: the special roof (and exact south orientation), special greenhouse, special south windows, etc. In a sense, the living region was regarded as secondary; in several respects it was required to conform to the solar design.

In designing Cliff House, the designer focused first on the living region. The solar heating system was made subservient: it was designed so as to suit the architect's and owner's wishes concerning the house proper.

In designing All-Solar-Too House, the designer gave approximately equal priority to the solar heating system and to the house proper. Also, great effort was made to keep the construction cost low.

Differences in Nominal Excess of Solar Capacity

Shrewsbury House was designed so as to have a nominal 40% excess of solar heating in a typical December (the most difficult month), i.e., a 40% excess if the builder did a perfect job of insulating and sealing the walls, roof, etc., if the December climate happens to be a *typical* December climate, and if the amount of intrinsic heat produced happens to be typical.

Cliff House was designed so as to have a nominal 20% excess—a margin that might not suffice if the insulation and airtightness fall appreciably short of specifications and if the December climate is exceptionally severe.

For All-Solar-Too House the nominal excess is about 30%.

Differences in Size of the Solar Staircase

Shrewsbury House employs a large (550 sq. ft.) Solar Staircase—for intake of much solar energy and for intense daylighting of the upper-story rooms via their ceilings.

Cliff House has no Solar Staircase. Solar collection is accomplished mainly by the sunspace.

All-Solar-Too House uses a small (100

sq. ft.) Solar Staircase; it is moderately helpful with regard to solar energy intake and daylighting.

Differences in Versatility of Controls

Shrewsbury House was designed for control by a single thermostat and a single fan. Adequate wintertime and summertime control of room temperature was achieved, but under some circumstances the control was only marginally adequate. Experimental use of an additional control has been initiated.

Cliff House and All-Solar-Too House have two thermostats and two fans, which provide closer, faster, and more positive control. Heating and cooling are controlled independently. The designer concludes that the slight extra cost involved is well worthwhile, especially as both fans usually operate at low power (25 to 50 watts).

Differences in Purpose of the Greenhouse

The Shrewsbury House greenhouse was designed for serious use in growing plants throughout most of the year (but not midwinter). The use of single glazing, combined with the high temperature and deep soil, has resulted in outstandingly fast rates of growth.

The Cliff House greenhouse—better called a sunspace—in intended to serve as an auxiliary living area, or lounge. Any use for growing plants is secondary. Use of double glazing, to save heat, slightly reduces the solation within the sunspace, thus slightly reducing the rate of growth of plants. Furthermore, there is no deep earth in the sunspace.

The All-Solar-Too greenhouse, only 8 ft. × 6 ft., serves mainly as an air-lock entrance.

Differences in Size and Cost

Shrewsbury House and Cliff House are large: they are two-story houses with all-inclusive floor areas of 2,860 and 3,200 sq. ft. respectively. The construction costs were in the neighborhood of $90,000 and $120,000 respectively.

All-Solar-Too House is small: one story, 1,000 sq. ft. It is expected that construction would cost about $50,000.

CRUCIAL NEW FEATURE COMMON TO ALL THREE HOUSES

The crucial new feature common to all three houses is the *opposed pair of room-temperature control capabilities*: ability to *raise* room temperature, and ability to *lower* room temperature.

At all times, these two capabilities exist, ready for prompt action. Even within a single day the system can supply both heating and cooling. No matter how suddenly the intensity of solation changes or how suddenly the outdoor temperature rises or drops, and no matter how greatly the rate of production of intrinsic heat increases (during a big party, for example) or how great a blast of cold air enters when someone accidentally leaves an outer door or window wide open for a half hour on a cold day—the simultaneous potentialities for supplying heating and cooling can overcome the difficulty.

The opposed-pair capability may be called a *two-way clamp*. The upper part of the south-attic thermal mass is at about 130°F and is ever ready to supply heat, and the lower part of the thermal mass below the first-story floor is at about 50°F and is ever ready to provide cooling. The attic system serves as a clamp to prevent drop in room temperature, and the below-floor system serves as a clamp to prevent rise in room temperature.

Notice the important benefit that the two-way clamp offers to the designer of a passive solar house: at once he is freed to employ a much greater amount of solar energy intake. Limitations on south window areas are relaxed. Huge areas may be used—areas so large that, for example, a nominal "140% passive solar heating" in December becomes a reasonable goal.

By way of contrast, note that the designer of conventional types of passive solar houses faces the dire threat of room overheating. He is safe enough as long as he plans on a mere 50% solar heating. But once he begins to plan for 75% or 90%, he faces near-insoluble problems. Suppose that, on a sunny day in October (when eave overhang is not effective, and when outdoor temperature may be high), room temperature rises to 90°F. What can be done? Not very much! Occupants can open

doors and windows, but this will not help much if the outdoor temperature is 85°F. And what if the occupants are all away? Remaining closed up, the house will stay warm for a very long time. Presumably it has large thermal mass; but, once heated to 90°F, such mass takes a very long time to cool off. Must air conditioners be provided?

Designers of superinsulated houses face a similar, but smaller, problem. Suppose such a house becomes too hot. What can be done? What can be done if the outdoor temperature is 85°F? What can be done if all the occupants are away?

Clearly, the trouble is that these types of passive solar houses lack a two-way clamp. In winter, such a house receives big "boosts" of heat; but it lacks cooling capability when needed. In summer, if the thermal mass has deliberately been kept cool, the house lacks means of supplying heat on, say, a cold cloudy morning. And between seasons, i.e., in spring and fall when a three-day sunny and warm period may be followed by a three-day cloudy and cold period, the house may successively lack cooling, then lack heating.

Because in winter such a house contains no provision against overheating, the designer must show great restraint in choosing the south window area. To seek 100% solar heating could be disastrous. The common advice is to provide enormous thermal mass (despite its various penalties), leave the floors free of rugs, provide thermal shades, instruct the occupants to open and close the thermal shades every day, warn the occupants to accept considerable excursions in room temperature—and seek only 50% to 75% solar heating and install an auxiliary heating system.

The restraint on south window area vanishes when the designer provides the two-way clamp. He is then free to use as large a south window area as he wishes. He is free to throw out the massive concrete walls and massive water-filled-container walls. He can let the occupants install as many rugs as they wish, and tell them to forget about thermal shade operation as no thermal shades are needed. And he can tell them to expect near-ideal temperature—in north rooms as well as south rooms, upstairs rooms as well as downstairs rooms.

In summary, the two-way clamp is much more than an incidental improvement, much more than an added gimmick. It opens up "a whole new ball game." It leads not just to 100% solar heating and elimination of the furnace, but to an increase in comfort and in simplicity of operation. Also, it permits wider choice of house shape, room layout, etc.

I consider the two-way clamp to be Saunders's greatest contribution to the art of solar heating.

The invention is magnified by various supporting strategies, such as:

- using direct passive collection and storage of solar energy, without need for intermediate heat-transfer processes that waste heat and are incapable of collecting and storing any heat at all on cloudy days.

- using a *huge* heat-exchange area between the storage system and the air that is circulated through it, so that heat exchange can be fast and efficient, airflow passages may be made generously wide, and a low-power fan suffices.

- using, in the storage-system heat-input process and heat-output process, airflow patterns that enhance the thermal stratification in the storage system.

- using various supplementary means of capturing solar energy.

- using integrated heat-recovery equipment, thus saving space and money.

- integrating the equipment for solar heating of domestic hot water so that no special collector or special insulation is needed and all of the heat that leaks out of the hot-water tank is recaptured for use in heating the rooms.

- integrating the system for control of glare, so that no special equipment is needed.

- relying mainly on "immortal" materials: air, water, stones, glass, fiberglass, concrete; no thin plastic sheets are used except in protected locations.

Note Concerning Solar Sandwich™

Saunders often uses the term *Solar Sandwich* to describe his designs that have both above-ceiling and below-floor storage systems. The term implies (rightly) that the living region of the house is sandwiched between two thermal storage systems.

A limitation of this term is that it fails to suggest the crucial function of the pair of storage systems: the two-way clamp. What is essential is that one storage system be hot and the other be part-near-70°F and part-well-below-70°F. Less essential is the sandwich geometry: one system above the living region, the other below.

ACCURACY OF "PERCENT-SOLAR-HEATED" PREDICTION

It is interesting that the only solar-heated houses for which one can make a perfectly accurate prediction of the *percent solar-heated* are those that are 100% solar heated. (More exactly: 100% heated by the combination of solar energy and intrinsic heat.) A house that has been designed for 100% solar heating with a reasonable margin of safety (reasonable nominal surplus) will indeed provide 100% solar heating. The uncertainty, or error, is zero.

Contrariwise, any house designed for, say 75% solar heating is likely to provide (because of the given imperfections in construction, the given set of occupants with their given lifestyle, and the actual climate in a given winter) anywhere from about 60% to 90%. The error can be large; the occupants face, at all times, uncertainty as to the amount of auxiliary heat that will be needed and the annual cost of such heat. Only when the house is designed for a 100%-plus margin does the uncertainty vanish—along with the annual heating bill!

One might argue: "If the percent solar-heated is high—that is, if the annual heating bill is small—who cares about the accuracy of predictions? Who cares whether the annual heating bill is $50 or $300? Any bill in this range is acceptable!" Such argument is on the whole valid. Note, however, that if the uncertainty extends over a range such as $50 to $300, many issues are left at loose ends. Designer A may claim his houses use only $50 worth of fuel per winter; designer B may claim a $200 bill for his houses—yet in fact his houses may use less fuel than designer A's use. In other words, the existence of such errors of predictions, claims, etc., makes it almost impossible to compare the various designs or the capabilities of various designers. Furthermore, one never knows whom to blame if actual fuel bills greatly exceed the predicted bills. Blame the designer for poor design? Blame the builder for poor construction? Blame the occupants for wasteful lifestyle and poor operation?

If, on the other hand, a house is designed for 100% plus a small margin, such uncertainties, doubts, and unanswered questions disappear. Provided that the builder did his job at least reasonably well and the occupants have reasonably favorable lifestyles, the fuel bill will be zero. There is nothing to argue about. Everyone is pleased. Everyone smiles.

IMPROVED DEFINITION OF PASSIVE SOLAR HOUSE

In the past, various definitions of *passive solar house* have been used. The most stringent is one requiring that no electrical power at all be used—not even power to run one small fan.

The time has come when the definition should be broadened to permit the use of fans for distributing heat. Today, the use of small fans to exhaust kitchen air and bathroom air is almost universal. Casablanca fans are often used to stir the living room air. Many new houses are so airtight that the use of air-to-air heat exchangers is necessary; a typical exchanger employs two fans. All such fans use, typically, about 25 to 150 watts, and the resulting bill for electric power comes to about $30 to $50 per year.

In houses that use fans for distributing heat, similar power levels apply—and similar annual bills. Thus the economic penalties (cost of fan, cost of power) are trivial relative to the benefits. Designers should not shrink from using fans in this low power range, and authorities on passive solar design should not exclude, from the *passive* category, houses that employ such fans.

The use of fans in the *collection* of solar energy is a very different matter. In cold winter weather, collection occurs typically only about 4 hours out of the 24. Thus the peak values of energy-collection rate are high, and the designer must provide a high-power (500 to 1,000 watt) fan or blower—almost ten times more powerful than the ones discussed above. Also, large airtight, well-insulated ducts are needed. The overall process is a major one, and rightly deserves to be called *active*.

But common sense justifies extending the use of the word *passive* to houses that employ low-power fans to vent stale air, circulate room air, or distribute heat. I regard the three Saunders-engineered houses described in this book as outstandingly successful *passive* solar houses.

CONCLUSION

The three houses I have described are real trailblazers. They are not perfect. They are not the last word. Further improvements will be made. But with their demonstration of the enormous power of the two-way clamp principle, their complete cutting loose from the furnace, and with their increased comfort and automatic operation, they are pointing the way toward a new era in house design.

PATENTS AND TRADEMARKS

PATENTS

Among the US patents obtained and owned by Norman B. Saunders are the following:

3,952,947	4/27/76	Solar heating system employing controlled introduction of outdoor air via a special window.
4,078,603	3/14/78	Skylight-type collector with storage and distribution systems.
4,123,002	10/31/78	System for controlling air temperature, humidity, and ventilation with use of ground coupling.
4,157,639	6/12/79	Seals for vertical and sloping windows or glazing.
4,201,189	5/6/80	South window solar radiation absorbing element (as in Shrewsbury House and All-Solar-Too House)
4,296,733	10/27/81	Transparent roof employing reflective louvers that admit much solar radiation in winter and admit little solar radiation in summer

He has other patents, but they have little or no pertinence to the houses discussed in this book.

Anyone contemplating using any of the devices, structures, etc., covered by one or more of these patents should direct inquiries concerning licenses and fees to Norman B. Saunders, 15 Ellis Road, Weston, MA 02193.

TRADEMARKS

Among the names trademarked by Saunders are:

Solar Staircase™

Heat Sandwich™

Dynamic Insulation™

North Window™

Air Gutter™

BIBLIOGRAPHY

C–85 Carriere, D., and F. Day. *Solar Houses for a Cold Climate*, Wiley & Sons, Toronto. 1980. 280 pp.

F–200 Fossel, P. V. "Engineered for the Sun," *Country Journal*, April 1983. p. 84.

G–182 Ghaffari, H. T., and R. F. Jones. *Thermal Performance of an Ekose'a Design Double-Envelope House*, published by Brookhaven National Laboratory, Upton, NY 11973. Report BNL 51518. June 1981. 162 pp. Price not indicated.

J–120 James, Russell. "Heating and Cooling on $50 a Year," *Mechanix Illustrated*, March 1983. p. 45.

R–190 Roberts, Raequel. "Automatic Solar House," *Handyman*, Sept. 1982. p. 136.

S–26 Saunders, N. B. *Solar Heating Basics*, 4th ed., published by N. B. Saunders, 15 Ellis Road, Weston, MA 02193. May 1976. 126 pp. $7.

S–27g ———"Performance of Solar Staircase™ Solar Heating System in Weston," Report of 10/19/76 to US Energy Research and Development Administration. P.O. WA–76–4947. About 30 pp.

S–27m ———"All Solar House 1981," 3rd ed., published by N. B. Saunders, 15 Ellis Road, Weston, MA 02193. 1981. 75 pp. $20.

S–235–t Shurcliff, W. A. *Solar Heated Buildings: A Brief Survey*, 13th ed. Published by the author from 19 Appleton Street, Cambridge, MA 02138. 330 pp. $12. Out of print.

S–235–aa ———*Solar Heated Buildings of North America: 120 Outstanding Examples*, Brick House Publishing Co., 34 Essex Street, Andover, MA 01810. 1978. 300 pp. $9.95.

S–235–cc ———*New Inventions in Low-Cost Solar Heating: 100 Daring Schemes Tried and Untried*, Brick House Publishing Co., 34 Essex Street, Andover, MA 01810. 1979. 296 pp. $13.95.

S–235–ee ———*Thermal Shutters and Shades: Over 100 Schemes for Reducing Heat Loss Through Windows*, Brick House Publishing Co., 34 Essex Street, Andover, MA 01810. 1980. 240 pp. $14.95.

S–235–ff ———"Underground Houses: Some Offhand Thoughts Against Them," *Earth Shelter Digest*, Sept.–Oct. 1980. pp. 27–29.

A–235–gg   ———*Superinsulated Houses and Double-Envelope Houses*, Brick House Publishing Co., 34 Essex Street, Andover, MA 01810. 1981. $13.95.

S–235–ii   ———*Air-to-Air Heat-Exchangers for Houses*, Brick House Publishing Co., 34 Essex Street, Andover, MA 01810. 1982. 200 pp. $12.95 paperback.

S–235–kk   ———"An Amazing Furnace-Free House," *Solar Age*, Nov. 1982. p. 33.

INDEX